DE VALERA'S FINEST HOUR

In Search of National Independence
1932-1959

De Valera's Finest Hour

In Search of National Independence 1932-1959

T. RYLE DWYER

THE MERCIER PRESS
DUBLIN and CORK

The Mercier Press Limited
4 Bridge Street, Cork
24 Lower Abbey Street, Dublin 1

ISBN 0 85342 675 9

To THERESE and all the Hassetts,
Michael, Matthew, David, Ruth,
John, Denis, Mary Lu, Paul,
Mark, Vera, Ed and Noel

PRINTED BY LITHO PRESS CO., MIDLETON, CO. CORK.

Contents

Acknowledgements

I would like to thank the staffs of the various institutions for their help, especially those at the Kerry County Library, Tralee; National Library of Ireland, State Paper Office, Trinity College, and University College, Dublin; National Archives, Washington, D.C.; Franklin D. Roosevelt Library, Hyde Park, New York; New York City Public Library; the Canadian Department of External Affairs and National Archives of Canada, Ottawa. I would also like to thank various people for their help and hospitality, my brother Seán and his wife Geraldine, Therese Hassett, Fr Anthony Gaughan, Michael Costello, Ger Power, John Lawlor, Joe O'Shea, Paddy Barry, Declan Keane, Tom Wallace and Bob MacSweeney. Finally I would like to thank my mother for reading the manuscript in all its stages and Mary Feehan for arranging its publication at very short notice.

Prelude[*]

In Dev's Darkest Hour

Throughout his political career Eamon de Valera was primarily concerned with securing complete national independence. He pursued his quest with such determination that he became the virtual personification of Irish independence. It was ironic that the American-born son of a Spanish father should be raised to such an exalted height, but then de Valera was a truly extraordinary person. To some he was a straight-forward individual with simple tastes, while to others he was an enigma, shrouded in mystery, and enclosed in a paradox.

Having come to power in 1932 he was depicted as both a staunch democrat and a would-be dictator, as an isolationist and an internationalist, as an enemy of the League of Nations and one of its staunchest supporters, as a puppet of the Irish Republican Army and its persecutor. He was really a very complex individual who could be all of those things. This work is not intended as a partial biography but an examination of his quest for national independence. This quest dominated his foreign policy during the most successful period of his political career when he dismantled the Anglo-Irish Treaty, won deserved international distinction at the League of Nations by pursuing statesmanlike policies, and successfully kept Ireland out of the Second World War while secretly rendering essentially all the help he possibly could to the Allies. Under his leadership Fianna Fáil won eight of the ten general elections it contested between 1932 and 1959, and in the process won outright majorities in the Dáil on four

---

[*] This prelude amounts to a brief summary of views put forward by the author in a separate book, *De Valera's Darkest Hour: In Search of National Independence, 1919-1932*.

occasions — a feat never even once accomplished by any of his opponents. Three of those four famous victories were attributable to his success in the quest for national independence. Whether one considers his contribution to Irish life as beneficial or malignant, there can be no doubt that he was the most important Irish politician in this century.

Being a divisive and contentious figure throughout most of his political career, it was ironic that de Valera first gained public prominence as a unifying figure. Following his release from jail in 1917 he managed to bring moderate and militant separatists together under the Sinn Féin banner by proposing they declare an Irish Republic and try to secure its recognition by appealing to the post-war Peace Conference. When recognition had been achieved the Irish people would then be free to determine their own form of government. Although he preferred the pacific route of securing diplomatic recognition, he left no doubt he was ready to endorse military measures, if necessary, to secure Irish independence.

As it became apparent that the approach to the Peace Conference was going to be futile, there were signs that young militants like Michael Collins were itching to provoke a violent confrontation with British authorities in the belief that Sinn Féin would gain by creating a state of general disorder throughout Ireland, but de Valera was not yet ready to abandon political means. He decided to go to America in an attempt to enlist sufficient popular support to compel the Washington government to endorse the Irish claim for self-determination.

While in the United States he exploited the controversy over possible American membership of the League of Nations and injected the Irish question into American politics by indicating Irish-Americans would support United States involvement in the League in return for formal recognition of the Irish Republic. Such tactics were deeply resented in Irish-American circles by isolationists, who were indignant at being depicted as ready to support American involvement in the League if Irish considerations were only satisfied. Leaders of the Friends of Irish Freedom (FOIF) made it clear they would not agree to

League involvement under any circumstances, and they resented de Valera's attempts to influence President Wilson by indicating to him that they and their supporters would accept policy which they had clearly indicated was unacceptable. De Valera's problems with the Irish-Americans really stemmed from a power struggle in which he insisted that he, as Irish leader, should have the final say on all matters relating to Ireland — even on the political tactics to be used by Irish-Americans in the United States—while FOIF leaders felt he should have no say in such tactics, as they were basically internal American political considerations.

The Irish-Americans undoubtedly had a legitimate grievance in view of de Valera's blatant interference in American affairs, but he could also feel justifiably aggrieved that they were only using the Irish question for their own political ends, especially when they took it upon themselves to speak out on essentially Irish matters and interfere in purely Irish affairs. A political truce was arranged in March 1920 with de Valera agreeing to keep out of American affairs while the others promised not to interfere in Irish matters. The President never really intended to uphold his end of the understanding. Having gone to the United States with the aim of enlisting enough public support to compel the America authorities to recognise the Irish Republic, he had no intention of staying out of American politics, especially in an election year. He was hoping to be able to secure a commitment from a presidential candidate to recognise the Irish Republic in return for the political support of Irish-Americans, but many Irish-Americans were not willing to allow themselves to be used in such a manner. Judge Daniel Cohalan, the effective leader of FOIF, was not prepared to back de Valera's efforts to secure a recognition plank in the Republican election platform at the party's National Convention in Chicago in June 1920. After the plank was rejected, de Valera deliberately undermined Cohalan's own efforts to get a differently-worded plank accepted.

Although the Irish leader publicly explained that he had undermined the Cohalan plank because it understated the

Irish case, this was clearly not the reason. He had really done so because he was afraid people might otherwise think he was merely a puppet of Cohalan. Some months earlier de Valera had written that he was afraid lest the 'judge would have the appearance in the eyes of the politicians of being the real power behind our movement — the man to whom they would have to go. Were I [to] allow myself to appear thus as a puppet, apart from any personal pride, the movement would suffer a severe blow.'[1] While it was noteworthy that he mentioned his 'personal pride' before referring to the interests of the movement, there could be little doubt that more than just pride was at stake; de Valera did genuinely believe the Irish cause would be best served if he were seen to be its undisputed leader. He therefore demonstrated his own supremacy, as he later admitted, by making it 'impossible for individuals in America to use the name of Ireland for any purpose but the one that Ireland wanted.'[2] In so doing he undermined what little chance there was of securing official American recognition.

Having complained that the United States was not big enough for Cohalan and himself, de Valera gave indications following his return home that Ireland was not going to be big enough for himself and Michael Collins, who had been one of the prime instigators in a campaign against British authorities, whose over-reaction — in the form of the Black and Tan terror — helped to generate the widespread disorder that Collins himself advocated provoking throughout Ireland back in March 1919. Having failed to despatch Collins to the United States in January 1921, the President soon became involved in a power struggle with him on the lines of the earlier one in the United States.

De Valera had been trying to pressurise the British into negotiating by issuing moderate statements and repeatedly emphasising his willingness to satisfy Britain's legitimate security needs, but his efforts were being compromised by the tendency of Collins to make hardline public statements. As a result the power struggle between them intensified. The President replaced Collins as deputy leader and then infuriated him by refusing to include him in the delegation that went to London for preliminary talks in July 1921. Yet Collins could not be ignored completely, as he had an enormous influence among the movement's militants and had also won the confidence of Arthur Griffith, who had a strong personal following among the more moderate political elements of Sinn Féin — the party he had founded and led for many years.

Realising it would be necessary to compromise if there was to be any chance of a settlement with Britain, de Valera was confronted with the dual problem of persuading the British to agree to acceptable terms and at the same time convincing radicals at home to accept the eventual compromise. His tactics were to remain in Ireland himself in an effort to persuade radicals like Cathal Brugha and Austin Stack to accept a compromise settlement, while he had his two strongest potential rivals within the movement, Griffith and Collins, selected to head the Irish delegation. He was trying to use them to persuade the British to accept his own compromise plan, External Association, which would accord Ireland the *de facto* status of the dominions without committing her to actual membership of the British Commonwealth. According to de Valera, the plan was designed to ensure that Ireland would legally have 'a guarantee of the same constitutional rights that Canada and Australia claimed.'[3]

For a time his tactics seemed to be working. In fact, during the final days of the London Conference, there was very little practical difference between what the British were demanding and what both the moderate and radical factions of the Dáil cabinet were prepared to accept, but this small difference was complicated by mutual distrust resulting from intensifying personality conflicts on the Irish side.

During the cabinet meeting that considered the British draft treaty on 3 December 1921, Brugha implied that Griffith and Collins were little better than traitors. For his part de Valera avoided personalities and concentrated his opposition to the British terms on the wording of an oath contained in the proposals. He later explained he wanted the plenipotentiaries to reject the draft treaty 'and see are the British going to make war on us because we won't give an oath to their King. Because that is what it amounted to.'[4] He suggested two or three alternative forms for the oath.

Back in London the plenipotentiaries signed the Treaty having secured some amendments, among which was a new oath that was comparatively similar to one proposed by de Valera, except that the latter had been thinking of External Association, while the new oath involved formally acknowledging membership of the British Commonwealth. De Valera was then presented with the Treaty as a *fait accompli* which he bitterly resented. He felt his efforts to maintain the tenuous unity between the factions within the cabinet had been destroyed. He had really done an excellent job of bringing the factions to the point where the whole cabinet was unanimously prepared to accept terms which were only symbolically different from what the British were offering. If he had been shown the Treaty before the signing, he said he could have tried to secure agreement within the cabinet. 'Had I seen it,' he told the Dáil, 'I would have used any influence I had to try to secure unanimity in the matter.'[5]

Notwithstanding the President's efforts to exonerate himself from any rersponsibility for what he saw as the fiasco caused by the signing, he must shoulder the bulk of the blame for what happened, because he was primarily responsible both for selecting Griffith and Collins to lead the delegation, and for insisting that they be given full plenipotentiary powers, although he knew they were contemplating a more moderate settlement than he had envisaged. When they eventually decided to sign the Treaty, they did so — not because of the ultimatum, which was issued only after Griffith had already committed himself but — because they believed that the terms would be acceptable to the majority at home, that those were the best terms they could get at the time, and that the difference between the terms offered by the British and what the cabinet was prepared to accept unanimously was not worth fighting over.

Collins realised there would be opposition within the

cabinet from 'those who have in mind personal ambitions under [the] pretence of patriotism.'[6] It was obvious that he considered de Valera among those individuals, and the President's subsequent actions undoubtedly confirmed those suspicions, at least as far as Collins himself was concerned. If de Valera had really felt as strongly about External Association, as he indicated in opposing the Treaty, it was really extraordinary that he hardly mentioned the issue during the cabinet meeting which considered the draft British terms. In fact, after more than six hours of discussion even Erskine Childers, who was deeply attached to the External Association plan, was unsure whether the President still wanted it. He therefore asked if in proposing the new oath de Valera also wanted the delegation to stand by External Association.

'Yes,' replied the President.[7]

Years later, having consulted his contemporary notes, Robert Barton explained that as far as he could remember, it was the only time during the whole meeting that de Valera referred to External Association.[8] Thus, if the plan was really so important, the President should certainly have made his views clearer. Collins, who for some reason did not hear Childers ask the question, actually left the meeting convinced that de Valera was prepared to accept the *de facto* status enjoyed by Canada, which was hardly surprising seeing that there was so little difference between that status and External Association.

During the Treaty debate in the Dáil de Valera admitted that the difference was very small, but he nevertheless insisted on proposing that his own alternative, Document No. 2, be substituted for the Treaty and presented to the British people in the hope that they would force their politicians to accept it. He was so taken with his own proposals that he seemed unable to believe that anyone could honestly prefer the Treaty. Consequently when Collins opposed Document No. 2 the President privately accused him of acting like Cohalan. And having come to look on him in the same light as the judge, de Valera apparently concluded that the Irish cause would be best served if the Treaty signed by Collins was undermined just as the plank

proposed by Cohalan had been undermined. Nevertheless
the scheme to get the British people to insist on the acceptance of Document No. 2 had little better chance of success
than the pathetic failure of the President's comparatively
similar effort in 1920 to get the American people to exert
political pressure on their government to accord official
recognition to the Irish Republic. Consequently, the Dáil
accepted the Treaty.

Having failed in the debate to regain the leadership role,
which he had effectively abdicated during the actual negotiations, de Valera was to encounter an even further loss of
influence in the hectic months that preceded the Civil War.
He did try to lead radical elements on a sane path by calling
for army unity after the Dáil approved the Treaty, by
denouncing talk of civil war, and by demanding that the
Irish people be consulted on the Treaty which, he contended, they had a right to accept even under the British
threat of war. But the more militant Republicans were unwilling to follow his lead in any of those matters, and de
Valera backed down on each of them. He called for the
army to divide on Treaty lines, talked rather recklessly
about the possibility of civil war, and demanded the elections be postponed for three months. On securing this
delay he found the militants were still not satisfied, and he
demanded a further delay of twice as long. When faced
with the blatant intimidation being used by Irregulars to
prevent elections, he publicly justified their actions by
declaring that there were 'rights which a minority may
justly uphold, even by arms, against a majority.'[9]

Some years later, having regained power, de Valera
behaved very differently on being confronted with the
same attitude which he had justified in 1922. 'If one section
of the community could claim the right to build up a political army,' he declared in August 1936, 'so could another,
and it would not be very long before this country would be
rent asunder by rival military factions.' He added that 'if a
minority tries to have its way by force against the will of the
majority it is inevitable that the majority will resist by
force, and this can only mean civil war.'[10] He was certainly
talking in very different terms than he had fourteen years

earlier.

In the interim, de Valera may have just changed his mind, but it seems more likely that what he said in 1922 was part of a desperate attempt to regain his waning influence among radicals in order to avert the calamity of civil war. At the time, he was vainly trying to lead supposed followers who were not really prepared to take their lead from him. On several occasions he, in effect, ran out in front of them, proclaimed where they should go, only to find they had marched on in a different direction. By repeating that process in his efforts to lead, he was really following the Irregulars as they brought the country down that same road which, he admitted in August 1936, could 'only mean civil war'.

In May 1922, de Valera did manage to negotiate the election pact which promised the possibility of re-uniting the movement. While it was generally seen as a victory for him, he did not see the pact in that light at all. In fact, he privately described it at the time as possibly being a 'slippery slope'.[11] He feared that candidates on the anti-Treaty panel of Sinn Féin would be defeated by pro-Treaty candidates representing the Labour Party, or standing as independents, which was what ultimately happened. There can be little doubt Collins violated the spirit of both the election pact by publicly intimating that voters in Cork should support pro-Treaty candidates outside Sinn Féin, and the spirit of the Árd Fheis agreement by only releasing the Constitution on the day before the election, with the result that critics had no real opportunity to explain its defects. By then de Valera's own hands were far from clean. He had already violated both the spirit and the letter of the Árd Fheis agreement by supporting those who were actively trying to prevent the June elections, and he had stood idly by while Republicans violated the terms of the election pact by intimidating independent candidates to prevent them standing in the election.

In the light of the plans and activities of those in the Four Courts, the Provisional Government's decision to clear out the building was understandable, but its decision to prorogue the Dáil for a couple of months was a different matter, especially as the pro-Treaty wing of Sinn Féin had lost its majority in the election. At the time de Valera was genuinely looking for a peaceful solution, although the other side could hardly be blamed for not trusting him. Moreover, he obviously had little influence on the Irregular leadership, which had repudiated all political control. He later regretted he had been 'so foolish' as to defend what he called 'Rory O'Connor's unfortunate repudiation of the Dáil', but de Valera had prepared the way for that repudiation himself by his own contemptuous attitude in walking out of the Dáil in protest against Griffith's election.[12]

Although widely depicted as the leader of Republican forces during the Civil War, de Valera had little real influence. It was Liam Lynch who called the shots. Todd Andrews, who acted as Lynch's adjutant, later wrote that as early as August 1922 de Valera realised there was no possibility of winning the struggle militarily. 'He wanted to call it off,' Andrews recalled, 'but Liam Lynch made it clear to him that any public action to this end would be repudiated by the Executive and the fighting would continue.'[13] Nevertheless de Valera did manage to get the Army Executive to agree to the establishment of an Emergency Government, which was formally set up by himself and just six other Republican members of the second Dáil. The Emergency Government was never much more than notional. As its President, de Valera had little real power. In February 1923, when he tried to suggest new proposals to end the Civil War, Mary MacSwiney objected on the grounds that he first needed the authorisation of the Army Executive, which he could not get because Lynch would not call a meeting lest the Executive would be persuaded to sue for peace by de Valera. When the latter suggested a settlement on the lines of Document No. 2, Lynch admonished him for bringing up old proposals. As a result de Valera was effectively hamstrung, and was unable either to bring up new proposals, or to resurrect old ones. It was only after the death of Lynch that he succeeded in persuading the army leadership to accept the proposals he had wanted to put forward in February.

Following the Civil War de Valera was leaning towards abandoning the Emergency Government before his arrest, but the set-up took a firm root among Republicans while he was in jail, with the result that after his release he again found himself in the position of having to follow hardline policies about which he had personal misgivings. He not only went along with the contention that the Emergency Government was the *de jure* government of the country, but he seemed to try to put himself out in front of the radicals by proposing the establishment of *Comhairle na dTeachtai* as the supposed *de facto* government. This move was most appropriately described by one close colleague as 'a lot of cods'.[14]

Although depicted by one biographer as presenting 'the slightly comic, slightly pathetic sight of the impractical idealist who tried to persuade himself and the world that he is a wholly practical man,'[15] de Valera really had to move slowly as he inched Republicans towards the constitutional framework of the Free State. Notwithstanding all the hyperbole about sacred principles, he admitted on numerous occasions that the unacceptability of the Treaty-oath was the only matter of principle on which he favoured abstaining from Leinster House. Opponents, on the other hand, maintained the oath was basically an empty formality, which de Valera belatedly discovered in 1927. Thus his opposition to the Treaty was not based on any principle but on what he apparently mistook for a principle. To some of the more cynical of his opponents, it seemed that he had no principles at all but was simply driven by a blind lust for power.

Shortly after coming to power in 1932 de Valera admitted he had underestimated the advantages of the Treaty.[16] Thus he, in effect, acknowledged that what he had called the 'small difference' between the Treaty and what he wanted, was even smaller than he had imagined.[17] Yet, for that smaller than 'small difference' he endorsed the actions of those who fought the Civil War rather than accept the Treaty. It should be emphasised that he did not instigate the civil conflict. It would have occurred whether or not he supported the radical Republicans, although many people were convinced it would not have been as drawn-out. Indeed one authority concluded that 'the Civil War would have been no more than a riot only for Dev's political cloak over it.'[18]

As radicals like Brugha, Stack and Mary MacSwiney had been prepared to accept Document No. 2, the realisation that the difference between it and the Treaty was even smaller than the 'small difference' originally envisioned probably only strengthened de Valera's conviction that the plenipotentiaries had made a tragic mistake in signing the Treaty. Had they followed his lead, he believed the Irish side would have preserved its unity and the British would have been faced with the decision of either accepting his terms or renewing the war for what would be, at most, only a smaller than 'small difference'. W. Alison Phillips, the eminent unionist historian, concluded a few years after that it was possible to regret that the British had not conceded what de Valera was seeking. 'To have done so,' he wrote, 'would not have exposed the Crown to any greater humiliation than it has suffered, nor Great Britain to any dangers from which the actual Treaty preserves her, while Ireland might have been spared the ruin, desolation and bloodshed of another year of fratricidal strife.'[19]

Had the Irish delegation held out for what the President wanted, the British might have ultimately conceded terms in line with Document No. 2. At any rate, de Valera believed they would, but those whom he had persuaded the Dáil to charge with the full responsibility of negotiating a settlement thought otherwise, and signed the Treaty. Since the plenipotentiaries had done what they perceived was their duty, de Valera was therefore largely responsible for what happened, because it was he who had insisted on full plenipotentiary powers being given to the delegation. He enjoyed an enormous facility for self-deception. He was apparently convinced that he had been blameless not only for what happened in London but also for all that subsequently happened at home.

There can be little doubt that de Valera was not guilty of all that he was accused of by his opponents, who posed as champions of law and order at the very time they impris-

oned him without trial, rather than charge him with the
only alleged crime of which they had any hard evidence —
specifically, that he had supposedly written an inciting
letter to the secretary of *Cumann na mBan* during the Civil
War. In spite of all the sonorous pronouncements about
standing for democracy, Griffith, Collins and their colleagues had flouted the very basis of representative democracy by proroguing the Dáil in the summer of 1922. While
they were no doubt exasperated by the utter contempt
shown for the principles of democracy by some of their
opponents, this did not justify ignoring the Dáil, especially
when their wing of the party did not have a majority in the
assembly. De Valera was actually so confident of the propriety of his own actions during the period that he later challenged W. T. Cosgrave to agree to an historical commission
to look into the causes of the Civil War, but the suggestion
was rejected contemptuously.

De Valera's opponents were so incensed at what they
saw as his treachery they really lost sight of what was supposedly their own ultimate goal — the Irish Republic.
Collins had, for instance, repeatedly stated that he accepted the Treaty only as a stepping stone to the Republic but,
as will become apparent in the following pages, most of his
supporters (while remaining ever ready to invoke his
name) seemed to forget about this afterwards as they concentrated on opposing the aims of de Valera, who actually
adopted the stepping stone approach himself. Ironically,
therefore, it was de Valera who eventually proved that
Collins had been right about the Treaty providing the
means to achieve the desired freedom.

In one respect, Collins was sadly mistaken. The Boundary Commission did not undermine partition, as he confidently expected. Of course, the Ulster question was not an
issue in the Treaty controversy between himself and de
Valera. The latter initially accepted the Treaty's partition
clauses, although he did subsequently argue that the Free
State would be cheated by the Boundary Commission.
When this transpired, the debacle helped to obscure just
how wrong he had been about the Treaty.

De Valera recovered from his tragic mistakes of 1921-22

by skilfully exploiting the Irish people's desire for independence. For generations all of Ireland's woes had been blamed on the British as the people were led to believe that independence would be a panacea. With the Free State's failure to meet the expectations of the people, many inevitably blamed the remaining British connection. Those people naturally turned to de Valera, who had consistently maintained that Ireland could never be independent until the last vestige of British sovereignty was removed. He never deviated from this line, which he at times espoused with the maddening self-assurance of what seemed like assumed infallibility. In the light of such consistency, his many inconsistencies were forgotten.

CHAPTER ONE

Proving Collins Right

Dismantling the Treaty

Following Eamon de Valera's accession to power as President of the Executive Council of the Irish Free State in March 1932 the British took the initiative in their relations with his government. J. H. Thomas, the Dominions Secretary, asked the Irish High Commissioner in London, John Dulanty, for clarification of Irish policy in view of the new President's recent campaign pledges to abolish the oath and withhold the land annuity payments.

De Valera, who personally retained the portfolio for External Affairs, obviously hoped to approach the contentious issues one at a time, for in his instructions to Dulanty he made no reference to the land annuities. The High Commissioner therefore avoided the question when he briefed Thomas on 22 March 1932. While the Irish government was determined to remove the oath, which he described as a 'relic of mediaevalism', Dulanty emphasised that Dublin was anxious for friendly relations with Britain, but he added that there could be 'no normal relations' between the two countries as long as the British government insisted upon imposing on the Irish people 'a conscience test which has no parallel in treaty relationships between states.'[1]

Thomas contended in reply that the oath was an integral part of the Anglo-Irish Treaty and could not therefore be abolished unilaterally. He also introduced the question of the land annuity payments, which he, in effect, linked with the issue of the oath by arguing that the Irish government was bound by the 'most formal and explicit undertaking to continue to pay land annuities.' Both issues were therefore covered by the sanctity of arrgement in the eyes of the British government.[2]

If there were any valid agreement regarding the payments, de Valera assured Thomas in reply that it would 'be scrupulously honoured,' but on the question of the oath he was not prepared to look on the Treaty as morally binding since Irish assent has been extracted under the threat of immediate and terrible war.

'Whether the oath was or was not an integral part of the Treaty made ten years ago is not now the issue,' he explained. 'The real issue is that the oath is an intolerable burden to the people of this state and they have declared in the most formal manner that they desire its instant removal.'[3]

During the election campaign de Valera had just argued that the oath had not been made obligatory, but having come to power he explained that he had never contended that 'the whole question' was to be determined on that argument.[4] He had simply omitted to elaborate previously that he was also relying on the Statute of Westminster, which guaranteed that the Free State and the other dominions could determine their own domestic policies. This statute therefore provided the authority to remove the oath, which formed Article 17 of the Free State's Constitution.

The Fianna Fáil leader's attitude during the election campaign was, of course, understandable. To have explained the situation fully would have meant highlighting one of the Cosgrave government's most impressive accomplishments, and he was not likely to win many votes by emphasising the achievements of his opponents, especially when those opponents had been unwilling to credit him with even basic integrity and had in fact engaged in a bitter campaign of villification against him.

On 20 April 1932 when the bill to remove the oath was introduced in the Dáil, it contained a provision doing away with the constitutional stipulation that no amendment would be valid which conflicted with the terms of the 1921 Treaty. In this way the danger that the Irish courts would overturn the abolition of the oath was minimised.

Explaining the legislation to the Dáil, de Valera stated that 'whatever the position may have been in 1921, in the year 1932 there is no doubt whatever that we can remove Article 17 of the Constitution, and do it without violating any contractual obligation whatever that we have with Britain.' As a result of the Statute of Westminster, which had 'been fully recognised by the British Parliament,' the dominions were officially recognised as 'co-equal partners' in the British Commonwealth. 'We are therefore,' he declared, 'today quite free to do anything here without any violation of the Treaty, anything that they can do in Canada, anything that they can do in Britain as regards our relations with the Crown.'[5]

While steering the bill through the Dáil, de Valera avoided further contact with the British on the land annuities question, but he did do some research into the matter after Thomas contended that the Free State was bound on the issue by two financial agreements drawn up with Britain in 1923 and 1926. The President was surprised by the mention of the former. It was the first he had ever heard of it, so he ordered a search for the document.

When found, the Irish copy of the agreement was in very poor shape. 'It is literally in tatters,' de Valera told the Dáil, 'half-pages, parts of pages not typed, interlineations and so on. Honestly, I never saw a contract of any kind presented in such a form. There is not even an Irish signature to it.'[6]

W. T. Cosgrave had signed the British copy of the agreement, but had never submitted it to the Dáil for ratification. The only form of confirmation to which the British could point was the rather extraordinary contention made by Thomas that the agreement had been ratified simply because Cosgrave had been returned to power at the next general election. One can sympathise with the observation that this was 'a novel constitutional doctrine for an English Minister to advance.'[7] It was preposterous to contend that the Irish voters had ratified an agreement, when they were ignorant of its very existence, not to mention its details. Even if the agreement had been binding, it was negated anyway by the terms of the Boundary Commission agreement.

The British realised that de Valera had a good case. On 8 March 1932, for instance, Neville Chamberlain, the Chancellor of the Exchequer, wrote that the Irish leader's stand on the Boundary Commission agreement 'might be regarded as an arguable point, if it is treated as a mere matter of legal interpretion of a particular phrase.' Chamberlain observed both that the wording of the agreement absolved Dublin 'from liability for the service of the Public Debt of the United Kingdom, and that the Irish Land Annuities form part of the Public Debt.' As a result he warned that there was 'a certain risk that an arbitrator might hold that Mr de Valera is right from a purely legal and technical point of view, and it would seem most undesireable that we should expose ourselves to such a decision.' It should be added, of course, that the chancellor was convinced that the Irish 'ought in equity to pay over the annuities,' and that 'they have clearly and definitely promised to do so.'[8] Although he did not appreciate the fact, it was a measure of justice that a rigid interpretation of the agreement abrogating the Boundary Commission should benefit the Free State, seeing that the country had lost so much from a similarly strict interpretation of the Treaty provisions providing for the Boundary Commission in the first place

The British argued that the Ultimate Financial Settlement of 1926 had subsequently bound the Free State to continue the land payments. Although that agreement was not ratified by the Irish parliament, Thomas pointed out that, unlike the 1923 agreement, it had been mentioned in the Dáil.

Upon taking a deeper look at the annuities question having come to power, de Valera said that he became more convinced than ever that the Free State was under no obligation to pay. 'Since we came into office with the responsibility which it involves,' he told the Dáil, 'we have given more detailed study to these matters than was possible when we were in Opposition, and the more we study them, the more we are satisfied that the position we took up in regard to them was sound both in law and justice.'[9]

His new found conviction was based in part on a fuller understanding of the relevant clause of the Ultimate Financial Settlement which read:

The Government of the Irish Free State undertake to

pay to the British Government at agreed intervals the full amount of the annuities accruing due from time to time under the Irish Land Acts, 1891-1909, without any deduction whatsoever whether on account of income tax or otherwise.

When taken with the 1923 agreement, about which de Valera had been ignorant before coming to power, it was obvious that the clause quoted above was really only dealing indirectly with the annuity payments by exempting them from Irish taxes to which they had previously been liable. Vice-President Seán T. O'Kelly observed therefore that the 1926 agreement was 'really irrelevant to the main question at issue,' but its citation by Thomas was indicative of 'the paucity of his arguments and the weakness of the British case.'[10]

De Valera never denied the existence of the financial agreements of 1923 or 1926; he simply dismissed them on the grounds that they had never been ratified. In short, his position was that financial questions which had not received parliamentary approval needed to be reconsidered, and he therefore invited the British to send representatives to Dublin for talks on the matter.

Few people could have missed the minatory significance of the make-up of the British delegation which visited Dublin in June 1932, as in addition to Thomas, there was the Minister for War, Lord Hailsham. If, however, the British thought that de Valera was going to be intimidated into submission, they were in for a sore disappointment.

The Irish leader, who characterised the talks as 'friendly discussions' rather than 'formal negotiations', was not in the least reticent about explaining his overall goals.[11] He said that his ultimate aim was to secure lasting peace and goodwill between Britain and Ireland. But he emphasised that this could only be accomplished if partition were ended and the island recognised as a republic. Once this had been done, he said that the new Irish state would probably be willing to form an association for external purposes with the British Commonwealth and would recognise the British King as head of the association. This, of course, was External Association all over again, so the British rejected it out of hand. For one thing Northern Ireland would undoubtedly be opposed to such an arrangement, and Thomas explained that no British government would 'ever attempt to coerce Ulster against her will.'[12] He also made it clear, however, that Britain would not compel the Twenty-six Counties to remain in the British Commonwealth.

'Don't think, Mr President, that the day you declare a republic you will be met by British guns and battleships,' Thomas said. 'You will be faced with the possibility of all your people in England being aliens — with the return to your country of thousands of civil servants and thousands of unemployed people now receiving public assistance. That will be Great Britain's answer, and it is for you to realise it. These facts should make people in both countries hesitate before they glibly talk of an Irish Republic.'[13]

In connection with the annuities, Thomas pointed out that the British intended to fulfil their commitments to those who had sold their lands. If the Irish government cut off the land payments, he warned that the London government would take 'whatever steps' were necessary to raise the money by other means. That was not intended as a threat, he told the House of Commons afterwards, but as a clear intimation that Britain intended to uphold her rights.[14]

The talks adjourned and reconvened in London the following week when Thomas suggested that the annuities issue should be submitted to a tribunal, as provided for by the Imperial Conference of 1930. De Valera was amenable to the idea but he insisted that the tribunal should not be limited exclusively to representatives from the British Commonwealth, because such a body would be biased in favour of Britain, seeing that all the other dominions looked to Britain as their mother country.

Upon his return to Dublin, de Valera secured governmental approval for the idea of submitting the financial issues to an international tribunal. He formally notified Thomas that the Free State accepted 'the principle of arbitration and agreed that a tribunal of a general character outlined in the report of the Imperial Conference, 1930, would be suitable,' but he added that his government could not agree to confining 'the personnel of the tribunal solely to citizens of the States of the British Commonwealth.' In addition, he also specified that 'in justice to the people of the Irish Free State' the tribunal should examine other payments that were being made to Britain by the Irish government without any formal parliamentary ratification of the two states.[15]

These proposals were literally ridiculed in the House of Commons. Members laughed as Thomas explained that de Valera intended that other questions, such as the over-taxation of Ireland during the nineteenth century, should be considered. Ridiculous as these proposals may have seemed to the British, de Valera was not prepared to surrender on either the financial or constitutional questions.

Although the Dáil had passed the bill removing the oath from the constitution with little difficulty, it ran into determined opposition in the Senate. While arguing for his bill on 25 May 1932, de Valera told the upper house that 'the only way' in which the Free State could be precluded from enacting the proposed legislation 'would be if the Treaty had fixed a position for all time out of which we could not advance from the point of view of status.'[16] Ironically, back in 1921 he had contended that the Treaty would bind the country to a fixed position while Collins and Griffith had argued that the state could evolve. Now de Valera was obviously taking their line, and their followers seemed blinded by annoyance. He was using the Statute of Westminster to achieve his own long cherished ends, although, while in opposition, he had not been willing to give them any credit for the major role that they had played in securing that statute, nor did he even admit at the time that it was of any particular importance. In fact, Fianna Fáil had opposed it in the Dáil.

But in June 1932 de Valera did admit to the Senate that developments within the British Commonwealth in the past decade had shown that he had underestimated the freedom conferred upon the Free State by the 1921 Treaty.[17] Some months later he told a British representative that he had initially feared that the Treaty would lead to British interference in Irish affairs, but he was since satisfied that the 'interference was very slight indeed.'[18] Those two occasions were the closest de Valera ever came to openly admitting that he had been wrong about the Treaty.

When the Senate refused to pass the bill removing the oath without first adding an amendment stipulating that the legislation would not come into effect unless the British and Irish governments could come to an agreement on the issue, the Dáil rejected the amendment and passed the bill in its original form on 12 July 1932. The Senate again insisted on its amendment eight days later, so the government had no real alternative but to let the suspensory period come into effect, which meant that the bill would become law in eighteen months, unless a general election intervened, which was of course what happened.

The oath, however, was not the only contentious issue involving the Free State's connection with the Crown. There was also Fianna Fáil's policy of minimising the role of the Governor-General by virtually ostracising him. The whole issue came to public attention in April 1932 when the *Irish Press* reported that two members of the Fianna Fáil government, Seán T. O'Kelly and Frank Aiken, had walked out of a social function at the French Legation in Dublin when the Governor-General arrived. At the time members of the government had been declining invitations to functions attended by the Governor-General, James MacNeill. O'Kelly and Aiken had not known that MacNeill had been invited when they went to the function in question, so in keeping with party policy, they withdrew upon his arrival.

MacNeill was incensed at the snub, which he considered a deliberate attempt on behalf of the government to insult his office. He therefore protested strongly to de Valera that the incident was 'part of a considered policy that the Governor-General should be treated with deliberate discourtesy by members of your Council and by the newspaper you control.'[19]

In reply, de Valera explained that 'the whole affair was unfortunate and regrettable, and should never have been allowed to occur.' Adding that MacNeill could feel 'justifiable annoyance' over the incident, the President went on to assure him that 'it was not part of a considered policy that the Governor-General should be treated with "deliberate discourtesies" either by members of the Executive Council or by the *Irish Press*.' Yet there was no hint or reproach, or criticism of O'Kelly and Aiken. In fact, de Valera obviously endorsed their action by suggesting that MacNeill should take steps to prevent any recurrence of the incident. 'If the Governor-General's public social engagements are communicated to me in advance,' he wrote, 'such an incident will certainly not occur in the future.'[20]

Dissatisfied with the reply, MacNeill demanded an apology from not only O'Kelly and Aiken, but also from de Valera himself, which drew a sharp response from the latter. 'In my previous letter to you,' the President wrote, 'I made it clear that I regarded the whole affair as unfortunate and regrettable, and one that should not have been permitted to occur. Further than this I am unable to go.'[21]

Matters were exacerbated during preparations for the Eucharistic Congress of June 1932 which was held in Dublin to commemorate the 1,500th anniversary of St Patrick's coming to Ireland. Before the change of government, MacNeill had invited some dignitaries to stay with him at his official residence during the Congress. When the Department of External Affairs subsequently explained that it would cause embarrassment to the new government if these dignitaries were guests of the Governor-General, the latter refused to withdraw the invitations. The government therefore took retaliatory steps. On learning that MacNeill and his guests were among those invited to attend a civic reception given by the Lord Mayor of Dublin, the Minister of Defence refused to allow the Army Band to perform for the occasion. And when a state dinner was held at Dublin Castle, neither the Governor-General nor any of his guests were invited.

There could be no doubt that MacNeill was being ostracised, so on 7 July 1932 he wrote to de Valera outlining the incidents that he considered deliberate insults on the part of the government. He had not sought his office, he explained, nor did he wish to retain it, if the performance of his duties were displeasing either to a majority of the Dáil or to the Irish people. 'But,' he added pointedly, 'I do not think I should resign any office because other office holders think I am a suitable target for ill-conditioned bad manners.' The Governor-General went on to warn that he had arranged for his letter and all the official correspondence with the President on the matter to 'be published within three days unless I receive apologies here from you and the other Ministers who have sometimes openly and sometimes otherwise sought to behave with calculated discourtesies to the Governor-General from whom you accepted confirmation of your appointments.'

The President immediately instructed MacNeill not to publish the correspondence, but when the time limit expired without any apologies being offered, the Governor-General ignored the instructions and released the letters to the press.

De Valera responded by demanding that the Governor-General should be relieved of his duties. At first the British asked for details of the dispute, but the President refused to furnish them. He was insistent that he should not have to explain his reasons, and the British conceded the point and agreed to the dismissal of MacNeill as Governor-General.

This was a concrete demonstration that the Irish Executive Council was in charge of the appointment of the Governor-General and that the King had to act on the advice of the Dublin government. Before nominating a successor, de Valera tried to minimise the significance of the post further by suggesting some alternatives. He proposed that the Chief Justice should assume the functions of the King's representative, without taking the Governor-General's oath of office, or else that the vacancy should be filled by a commission of three — one of whom would be the President himself.[22]

For some days rumours abounded. There were suggestions that de Valera was simply going to combine the office with his own, or that he was about to appoint a washerwoman to the post.

But when the British rejected his suggestions, the Executive Council advised that Domhnall Ó Buachalla, a retired shopkeeper and a twice defeated Fianna Fáil candidate for the Dáil, be appointed Governor-General. He did not take up residence at the Vice-Regal Lodge, but moved instead into a house in the Dublin suburbs, where his sole official function was to affix his signature to acts of the Irish parliament.

Meanwhile the dispute over the land annuities and other payments came to a head with the British on 1 July 1932 when the Dublin government defaulted on its payment. The British responded by getting parliament to authorise the levying of custom duties on imports from the Irish Free State as a substitute means of collecting the money.

As those measures were sure to have a serious effect on the Irish economy, de Valera made it clear that he was anxious to avoid a confrontation. He announced that he had already ordered that the disputed payments should be lodged in a suspensory account until the problems could be settled by negotiations, and he suggested a meeting with Prime Minister Ramsey MacDonald to discuss the whole affair. A meeting was therefore duly arranged for 15 July 1932 in London.

During that meeting de Valera advocated that if the British were not prepared to accept the arbitration of an international — as opposed to imperial — tribunal, the two sides should try to settle the financial question by bilateral negotiations. He added, however, that until such negotiations could be held, the British should suspend the implementation of the retaliatory tariffs recently approved by parliament, which were due to come into effect the following day. Otherwise, he warned that the British measures would lead to counter measures by the Dublin government and that the resulting climate would be inconducive to fruitful negotiations.

Prime Minster MacDonald agreed that the matter should be settled by negotiations but he went on to insist on the rather extraordinary preconditon that 'if there was to be a suspension of the duties there ought to be a complete return to the *status quo* which the Irish Free State Government had been the first to disturb.'[23] In other words, Dublin should immediately make the defaulted payments, which of course de Valera refused to do.

Next day customs duties, amounting to twenty per cent *ad valorem,* were duly levied on imports from the Free State, and the Dublin government responded by imposing comparatively similar import duties on British goods. So began the economic war that was to continue for almost six years as measures met with counter measures.

When Thomas suggested that the two sides should start negotiations without a tariff truce, de Valera agreed and went to London for talks during mid-October 1932, but nothing came of them. The problem was basically that the British were trying to get de Valera to back down on his approach to constitutional matters, especially the oath, on which he was unwilling to budge, while the Irish leader was trying to get the British to agree to arbitration on the financial issues on which they were not prepared to compromise unless he first conceded. They told de Valera that he should abandon the attempt to remove the oath and accept that the 1923 and 1926 financial agreements were binding. Then in return, they would discuss a modification of the oath and the mitigation of the financial payments, in addition to offering to negotiate a trade agreement.[24]

Although Thomas stated that the financial and constitutional issues were separate, the British tended to view both issues as basically part of the over-all constitutional problem once de Valera insisted on going outside an imperial tribunal for arbitration. Sir Thomas Inskip, the Attorney-General who had sat in on the meeting between Mac-Donald and de Valera, admitted that the constitutional question was really Britain's prime consideration, and he added that if it were not for it, there would be little difficulty in overcoming the other issues.

'If there could be a clear and sincere declaration of the desired intention of the Irish Free State to stay within the Empire on the basis of their constitutional position and in a spirit of loyal partnership,' Inskip said, 'no annuities or debts could cloud the prospect.'[25] The Dominions Secretary himself conceded some time later that Britain would have little difficulty in getting over the annuity question, 'if that were the only matter in dispute.' He made it clear that the constitutional issues were the fundamental problem.[26]

Thus an impasse was reached, because de Valera was unwilling even to discuss the question of the oath, which he felt was basically an internal matter which the Statute of Westminster had empowered his government to deal with as the Irish people saw fit. Subsequently the highest British authorities admitted that de Valera's assumption was basically correct all along. But in the interim the British government adopted such an intractable stance on the financial question that the Irish leaders suspected that some sinister encouragement was coming from discontended Irish elements.

'I have come to the conclusion,' he told the Dáil on 19 October 1932, 'that the British Government, pressed forward as it is by certain anti-Irish feeling in Britain and supported by the attitude of a minority in this country, is not prepared to examine this position on its merits or to yield to claims of simple justice.'

As he did not specify just what Irish minority was acting so unpatriotically, Cosgrave asked for clarification of the remark.

'A minority is a minority,' de Valera replied curtly, 'and those that the cap fits can wear it.'

There could be no doubt that the President was holding the opposition partly responsible for the failure of the London talks. Whether or not such a charge was justifiable may be open to question, but there can be no doubt that the British were encouraged in their intransigence by the hope of an early general election that would lead to Cosgrave's return to power.

Paradoxically even though Michael Collins had made it clear that he accepted the 1921 Treaty only as a stepping stone to more complete freedom, some of his followers were later to invoke his name in support of the agreement as if it were intended as a permanent settlement. Having fought against those who were trying to wreck the Treaty, they became inflexible in their support of the document. They were determined to prevent de Valera achieving in 1932 what he had failed to do in 1922.

Fionán Lynch, a former minister in the Cosgrave government and one of the four secretaries who had accompanied the Irish delegation during the London Conference of 1921, gave a vivid example of the Treatyite intransigence in a letter he wrote to his local newspaper in August 1932.

'Those who supported the Treaty in 1922,' he wrote, 'and those of us who fought to maintain it, will consider ourselves traitors — traitors to the memory of Collins and O'Higgins and of the scores of National Army men who gave their lives that the Treaty might be secured for the people of this State — when we desert that cause that they died for and go over to those who were responsible for their deaths.'[27] The bitterness of the Civil War was so intense that people were losing sight of their original goals and opposing what they once had favoured, simply because their opponents favoured the same thing.

If Collins was honest in advocating that the Treaty should be used as a stepping stone — and there seems no reason to doubt that — then Fionán Lynch and others, who so readily invoked their former leaders's name, actually abandoned his cause. The difference between Collins and de Valera in 1922 had not been over ends, but means. They both shared the common ultimate goal of securing an all-Ireland republic, but Collins thought that the best way of securing it was to accept the temporary inconvenience of the Treaty on the grounds that it provided the best means of developing the desired freedom.

One opposition journal actually acknowledged the compatability between the part played by de Valera and the role advocated by Griffith and Collins. The *United Irishman** explained, for example, that the latter pair had signed the Treaty in the belief that the status of Canada was a basis on which Irish institutions could be built and expanded. Collins had repeatedly emphasised that the country could progress with Canada towards complete freedom and even hasten the pace. The editor therefore concluded that 'No men have paid greater tribute to the way in whichthe Treaty has been enlarged and improved than President de Valera and his Attorney-General.'[28]

Notwithstanding the constitutional progress that de

* Should not be confused with the subsequent Sinn Féin organ of the same name.

Valera was making, he was running into difficulties from impatient republican elements, who were allowed a much freer rein under his government. They actually tried to exacerbate the economic war by calling for a boycott on all British goods. Walls throughout the country were inscribed with the slogan, 'Burn Everything British But Their Coal.' Not being content simply to encourage the boycott by peaceful means, these republican elements resorted to violence and intimidation.

Bass Ale was a favourite target of these radicals, who warned publicans not to stock the British beer. One consignment coming from the Dublin docks was actually hijacked and dumped into the River Liffey. The Dublin Beer Party, as the incident was dubbed by republican propagandists, was supposed to be a symbolic re-enactment of the famous Boston Tea Party on the eve of the American Revolution.

Threats against the supporters and members of the previous government were even more serious from the political standpoint. Their meetings were being forcefully disrupted by republicans, who were demanding that there should be no free speech for traitors. These disruptions gave rise to the growth of the Army Comrades Association, the strength of which grew from about 7,000 members to around 100,000 within a few months, as the association pledged itself to prevent disruptions of public meetings.

De Valera personally denounced the attacks on his opponents and called on members of Fianna Fáil to avoid involvement. 'I want everyone in our organisation to have nothing to do with intimidation of other people or with the interference at public meetings,' he told the party Árd Fheis. 'Anyone who tries to intimidate his opponents is simply showing that he himself is afraid of something. We are not afraid of anything because we believe we are truly representative of the desires of the Irish people.'[29]

By late 1932 there were signs that the opposition elements were coalescing. James Dillon, the independent deputy who had supported the election of de Valera as President, for example, helped to found the National Centre Party, and was gaining significant support among the farming community, which had been most seriously affected by the economic war. In addition to hardships caused by the disastrous drop in cattle exports, there was discontent over the land annuity question. Some people had thought that de Valera had been promising to abolish the annuities, whereas in fact he had only proposed withholding them from the British pending re-negotiation. He still intended that the Land Commission would continue to collect the annuities from farmers.

Dillon and Frank MacDermot, another principal founder of the new party, entered negotiations with the Cosgraveites with a view to uniting politically, but before they could combine effectively, de Valera called a general election for January 1933.

During the election campaign Fianna Fáil emphasised the Opposition's failure to support the government in the struggle with Britain, and this was depicted as a lack of patriotism. Although Cumann na nGaedheal ran a more positive campaign this time, it seemed to be simply trying to outflank Fianna Fáil by adopting modifications of de Valera's own policies. For instance, Cosgrave promisd that if he got back into power, he would cancel arrears in land annuity payments, declare a moratorium on their payment for 1934, and would negotiate to have them reduced thereafter. He also promised to end the economic war, arrange for a trade agreement with Britain, and secure a revision of the financial agreements by 'courageous negotiations.'[30] The overall programme prompted de Valera's supporters to declare that 'even Cosgrave admits that Fianna Fáil was right all the time.'[31]

Fianna Fáil duely increased its share of the seats in the Dáil and won an outright majority of its own. Although it was the slimmest majority possible 77 out of 153 seats — the party could still rely on the support of the Labour Party. De Valera was therefore easily re-elected President, and he again retained the portfolio for External Affairs. According to his biographers, 'he always felt that this was a post which should, if possible, be held by the Head of Government, so that there might be no doubt as to the authority with which the Minister spoke.'[32]

One of the really striking features of the previous year in office was the strong personal control that de Valera retained over the country's international negotiations. Although he often brought colleagues into the various diplomatic talks, he changed them around so much that none ever had a chance to acquire real competence in the area.

When Thomas and Hailsham came to Dublin for talks in June 1932, for instance, de Valera was accompanied by James Geoghegan, the Minister for Justice, and by the Attorney-General, Conor Maguire, but when the talks reconvened in London three days later he brought Vice-President Seán T. O'Kelly. And when he returned to London the following month to meet MacDonald, he was accompanied only by a secretary. Of course, at the same time O'Kelly and two other senior colleagues, James Ryan and Seán Lemass, the respective Ministers for Agriculture, and Industry and Commerce were bound for the Imperial Economic Conference in Ottawa. But when the talks with MacDonald failed, the President instructed the delegation not to partake in the Ottawa conference. During September he took Joseph Connolly, the Minister for Post and Telegraphs, to Geneva. Then on the way home when he stopped off in London for talks, he was joined by Conor Maguire, the Attorney-General. And on returning to London for formal talks with the British a fortnight later, he brought Geoghegan, Maguire, and Seán MacEntee, the Minister for Finance. By involving so many ministerial colleagues, de Valera undoubtedly strengthened his own hand within the Executive Council on matters relating to External Affairs. He kept the cabinet well briefed on the negotiations with the British, and reports of the talks were given to all cabinet members. Since so many of the ministers were themselves involved in the discussions, the cabinet could rest assured that it was being kept fully informed, yet none of the ministers was given the opportunity of gaining enough experience or expertise to be regarded as competent to challenge de Valera's authority in the negotiations.

Once re-elected in February 1933, the President was

again faced with the issue of the oath, seeing that the bill removing it had been invalidated by the holding of the general election. The bill was therefore re-introduced in the Dáil, where it passed easily, but it was refused a second reading in the Senate, which adopted a resolution instead calling on the government to seek an amicable agreement on the issue with Britain. The Senate's action — in simply refusing to act on the bill, rather than formally rejecting it — meant that it would become law within sixty days, instead of having to wait for the suspensory period of eighteen months. Thus the legislation formally became law on 3 May 1933.

By that time de Valera had already reiterated the policy he had outlined at the inaugural meeting of Fianna Fáil by making it clear that the removal of the oath was only the first step of a strategy to dismantle systematically all of the disagreeable aspects of the 1921 Treaty. Speaking at Arbour Hill on 23 April 1933 he explained that he was not prepared willingly to 'assent to any form or symbol' that was incongruous with the country's status as a sovereign nation. 'Let us remove these forms one by one,' he said, 'so that this State that we control may be a Republic in fact and that, when the time comes, the proclaiming of the Republic may involve no more than a ceremony, the formal confirmation of a status already attained.'

De Valera's next major move towards dismantling the Treaty was undertaken the following August when his government introduced three bills limiting the constitutional connection with the British Crown. The first two bills curtailed the powers of the Governor-General, both by transferring to the Executive Council his nominal power of recommending the appropriation of money bills, and by abolishing his authority to withhold the King's assent to bills and thus reserve them for the signification of the King's pleasure. The third piece of legislation abolished the right of appeal to the judicial committee of the Privy Council. All three bills became law in mid-November 1933.

The Dublin government had clearly acted within the authority conferred by the Statute of Westminster. But Thomas made the rather extraordinary accusation in the

House of Commons on 14 November 1933 that the bills
were a violation of the Treaty. He went on to warn that the
gradual elimination of the Crown from the Irish constitution would lead to the withdrawal of those benefits enjoyed
by the Irish Free State and its citizens as a result of the
country's membership of the British Commonwealth.

The Dominions Secretary's remarks brought up the
whole question of whether continuing Irish membership of
the British Commonwealth was one of free choice or com-
punction. De Valera, ever mindful of the way in which the
Treaty was forced upon the Irish people, noted that the
country had been compelled to accept membership of the
British Commonwealth under threat of war, which was of
course contrary to the concept of equal partnership. He
therefore asked for an assurance that if the Irish Free State
withdrew from the Commonwealth, Britain would not
resort to waging 'war or other aggressive actions' against
the Irish.[33]

The British initially intended to provide the requested
assurance tempered with a warning on the lines of that
given by Thomas in June 1932 when he told de Valera that
if the Free State withdrew from the Commonwealth, the
Irish people in Britain and the Dominions would become
aliens with all the disadvantages that this would entail, such
as the necessity of registering with the police, liability to
deportation, denial of the franchise and the various restrictions that would be placed on their employment in areas
like the civil service. But Thomas feared that reiterating his
warning formally would only make matters worse,
especially if de Valera tried to make political capital out of
it. The British therefore drafted a vague reply expressing
disbelief that the Dublin government would ever consider
withdrawing from the Commonwealth and thus refusing to
forecast Britain's attitude in such a hypothetical situation.

Although de Valera's moves towards dismantling the
Treaty were of necessity essentially unilateral, he remained
mindful of the influence of American public opinion,
especially as a deterrant to any rash actions that the British
might contemplate. Thus he was disturbed in late 1932
when there were signs that the British were actually

enhancing their public image in the United States at the
expense of the Irish by successfully equating the Dublin
government's refusal to pay the land annuities with the
defaulting by some countries of their war debt payments to
the United States.

The war debts issue was a particularly emotive one in the
United States in December 1932 when France, Belgium,
Poland, and Hungary defaulted on their American payments. Against that backdrop the British received favourable press coverage when they turned over their payment
of $95.55 millions in gold, especially as the British govern-
ment was strapped for money at the time. Neville Chamberlain explained to parliament having made the American
payment that a supplementary budget was necessary
because the country's unemployment relief had cost more
than was expected, and the anticipated Irish land annuity
payments had not been received.

Next day the Irish role in the affair was blown out of all
proportions by a front-page headline in the *New York
Times*, which declared that 'Irish Land Issue and Relief Put
Britain Out £21,420,955.'[34] From the headline it appeared
that the lost Irish revenue made up a substantial part of
Britain's shortfall, whereas it only amounted to £3.41 millions, with the remainder being due to unemployment relief
paid out in Britain.

Faced with the possibility of a serious erosion of American sympathy, de Valera moved swiftly to counteract the
situation. He set out to draw a stark contrast between the
Irish Free State and the war debt defaulters by announcing
that the Dublin government was making arrangements to
repay all money loaned by Americans during the bond-
certificate drives of 1920 and 1921. In that way it was possible to depict the Irish among the very few people to repay
what amounted to a war debt to the United States.

There was also undoubtedly a further angle in de
Valera's thinking. Franklin D. Roosevelt, the New York
lawyer who had advised him on the legality of the bond-
certificates in 1919, had recently been elected President of
the United States, and he would likely take particular
notice of the repayment gesture.

De Valera sent Joseph Connolly, his Minister for Posts and Telegraphs, to the United States to make the necessary arrangements for repaying the money still outstanding which, together with a 25% premium, amounted to less than four million dollars, because fifty-eight cents on the dollar had already been returned as a result of the litigation in the 1920s. The remainder, together with the premium, was to be paid in cash and stock to bond-certificate holders.

Connolly deliberately exploited his trip to play up the contrast with those countries who had defaulted. 'We have read in Ireland of statements which seemed to aim at creating the impression in the United States that we are a nation of defaulters,' he told a New York press conference. 'Nothing is further from the truth. We are not defaulters and my visit here, to confer with our representative in the United States on the arrangements to pay voluntarily the 1920-21 Republican bonds issue, is ample evidence of that fact.'[35]

'The American press and people appreciated the ironical contrast,' Connolly later wrote, 'and I make no apology for exploiting the situation to the full.'[36] He even managed personally to make sure that Roosevelt was aware of the Irish gesture, by securing a meeting with the President a few days after the latter's inauguration. According to Connolly, the American President was interested in Anglo-Irish relations because of their impact on American politics. In view of the political influence of Irish-Americans, Roosevelt noted that Irish hostility towards Britain 'was not going to help to any understanding between Britain and the United States.'[37]

There was one example of cordial Anglo-American relations, however, that was leading to a certain amount of uneasiness in Dublin, where Irish authorities were far from happy with Frederick Sterling, the first United States Minister to the Free State. He was considered too pro-British and he irked Irish officials by spending much of his time in London. The ultimate indignity was when he tried to secure diplomatic standing for his London apartment. Fearing that this would lead Washington to decide that its ambassador in London could effectively combine the

British and Irish positions, Dublin balked at Sterling's request and let the press know that he was looked upon with disfavour. He was duly transferred to Bulgaria in the moves that followed the change of adminstrations in Washington, D.C.

When Sterling's replacement, William W. McDowell, took up his post in Dublin some months later de Valera used the occasion to further demonstrate his own determination to remove the symbols of Britain's dominion over Ireland. In accordance with protocol McDowell's credentials were addressed to King George V, so it made front page news in the United States when he presented them to de Valera, rather than to the Governor-General as had been customary. The State Department, which only learned of the affair from the press, was taken aback, especially as there were reports that Vice-President O'Kelly had made a hardline speech in Dublin later that evening.

'One by one we are cutting the ropes and chains England has wound around us here,' O'Kelly told a Fianna Fáil gathering. 'Every day something is being done to oust the British from control in our country.' He added that if necessary the government would resort to force and use the Irish army. 'We will,' he emphasised, 'use every effort to re-establish the republic for the thirty-two counties.'[38]

Although it initially appeared that the Irish had used the arrival of the new America Minister to deliver a calculated insult to the British king, McDowell assured Washington that the procedure of bypassing the Governor-General had been approved by the British in advance. He subsequently reported that he was later shown a letter, initialed by King George V himself, approving of the arrangement.[39]

The Irish minister in Washington approached Secretary of State Cordell Hull in an effort to get the State Department to publish a full explanation of the affair. But Hull was reluctant to become embroiled in any Anglo-Irish matters. He had already committed a *faux pas* some months earlier when, on stopping at Cobh on his way to the World Economic Conference in London, he proposed a toast to the 'Irish Republic'. Once he learned that the King had authorised the change in procedure, he was unwilling to become further involved, and ordered that the matter should be considered closed.[40]

Nevertheless the whole affair received further publicity less than a fortnight later when McDowell dropped dead in Dublin Castle at a state dinner welcoming him to Ireland. At the time that he was striken by a fatal heart attack, he was actually responding to a toast to his health made by de Valera. In view of the ironic circumstances, his death received extensive publicity in the United States, where newspapers naturally referred back to events surrounding the presentation of credentials twelve days earlier.

Following the further minimisation of the functions of the Governor-General, de Valera's next move in his systematic dismantling of the disagreeable aspects of the Treaty was to introduce legislation giving effect to his concept of 'reciprocal citizenship' first advocated in 1921. The move was embodied in three separate pieces of legislation that were introduced simultaneously. The first, the Citizens Act, defined Irish citizenship and purported to deprive Irish people of being British subjects. The Aliens Act, on the other hand defined British subjects as aliens in Ireland, while the third bill removed the practical difficulties that the new legislation created for British subjects. In other words, the British were defined as aliens but were to be treated as if they were Irish citizens. De Valera had thereby secured one of the most fundamental aspects of External Association.

By the time the bills became law in 1935 there had been a further development in Britain that eliminated any confusion about the legality of the Irish government's unilateral dismantling of the Treaty. In its findings on a case questioning the Irish government's abrogation of the right of appeal to the judicial committee of the Privy Council, the committee itself found that while the Irish had no authority to abrogate the Treaty prior to 1931, the Statute of Westminster had thereafter conferred the necessary power. Thus, the British thereby admitted that Dublin did indeed have the authority to abolish not only the right of its citizens to appeal to the Privy Council, but also the oath prescribed in the Treaty.

Although the decision of the judical committee undermined part of the British case in the continuing dispute with the de Valera government, it did not of course affect the broader aspects of the economic war, which had been continuing with growing intensity, but there were signs of an uneasiness in certain British circles. In September 1934 the *Manchester Guardian* denounced the London government for 'a supineness without modern parallel' because of its failure to negotiate an end to the trade war.[41] This was followed seven weeks later by similar criticism in *The Economist*. 'The damage to Ireland is clearly large,' it noted, 'though apparently by no means as catastrophic as the British government expected. The damage to Great Britain is no less. Our best customer has fallen to fifth place; our shipping, insurance, and other "invisible" income has been diminished.' *The Economist* went on to state that if Britain were engaged in a trade war with Germany, France, or the United States, there would be a clamour for government action. Yet prior to 1932 Britain's trade with the Irish Free State had been more valuable than with any of the great powers. Thus, the influential journal concluded, 'if the British public allows the economic war with the Free State to continue, it does so in ignorance of the magnitude of the issues involved.'[42]

Within a matter of days the first cracks in the British resolve to pursue their economic campaign with full vigour began to appear when for purely business reasons, a coal-cattle agreement was concluded with the Irish. John Dulanty, the Irish High Commissioner in London, had taken the initiative of approaching the British after Irish representatives had begun investigating the feasibility of using German and Polish coal rather than the supplies normally acquired from Britain. As this would have entailed costly alterations to Irish industrial plants in order to make the transition to the different type of coal, the British were confronted with the possibility of losing their Irish coal market permanently, because once the Irish industries adapted themselves to continental coal, they would be reluctant to incur further costs in changing back after the economic war. The British therefore agreed to a deal in accordance with which they would buy more Irish cattle and the Irish would import more British coal.

The most significant improvement in the British attitude did not occur, however, until 1936 after Malcolm Mac-Donald had taken over from J. H.Thomas as Dominions Secretary. With one eye on the deteriorating international situation, as Germany was rearming and Italy was acting aggressively, MacDonald argued that it was in Britain's interest to settle the dispute with de Valera. He explained, for example, that such a settlement would not only strengthen Britain's standing in world affairs, but would also improve her defence posture, and materially assist British trade and industry. Moreover he noted that the Irish were obviously moving towards the introduction of a new constitution in which the King would only be recognised for external purposes, which meant that 'all hope of keeping the Free State in the Empire would be at an end.'[43]

After some secret informal meetings with de Valera, MacDonald suggested that Britain should take the initiative in starting comprehensive negotiations with the Dublin government in an effort to settle the constitutional, economic and the defence issues that were raised by Britain's retention of Irish ports. He proposed that the British authorities should take the first step by formally acknowledging that the Irish Free State was mistress of her own destiny and that while Britain would deeply regret the Free State's withdrawal from the British Commonwealth, the Irish were perfectly free to leave, if they wished. As the proposals were awaiting consideration, de Valera informed the Dominions Office of his plans to introduce a new constitution. He explained that while the affair was really of no concern to the British, he was informing them anyway as a matter of 'courtesy'.

MacDonald was authorised to engage in further talks with de Valera, so several meetings followed between the two men. Although these were cordial, the Irish leader was unwilling to abandon his plans to introduce External Association which, he said, was as much as his government could concede to British sentiment. He argued that his plans were not incompatible with membership of the British Commonwealth, but if the British thought otherwise, they would have to expel the Free State. In short, he was going to press ahead with his plans whether the British liked them or not.

For their part the British were diligently trying to find a way to persuade de Valera to remain in the Commonwealth, but they could see no hope if his government renounced allegiance. MacDonald and his cabinet colleagues seemed mesmerised by the whole allegiance issue. They were insistent that Dublin would have to retain the common bond that was involved in full allegiance to the Crown, if the Free State were to remain part of the Commonwealth.

Confronted with other major problems, the British thought that they had plenty of time to find a settlement with de Valera before the new constitution could be introduced. In November 1936, for instance, de Valera told a Fianna Fáil Árd Fheis that the necessary legislation would not be ready until the new year. But when the controversy arose over the abdication of King Edward VIII, the Irish leader moved swiftly. He co-operated with the British in the implementation of the abdication act, but in so doing he seized the opportunity to enact legislation that formally eliminated the new King from the internal affairs of the Free State.

The External Relations Act, which was introduced on 11 December 1936, was passed with full speed the following day. It stipulated that as long as the Irish Free State was associated with such dominions as Australia, Canada, Great Britain, New Zealand, and South Africa, and so long as they recognised the British King 'as the symbol of their co-operation' in matters like the appointment of diplomatic and consular representatives, the Executive Council had the authority to advise the King to act on the Free State's behalf in such matters. It should be emphasised, however, that the wording of that legislation was such that the King could only act on the advice of the Executive Council and even then, the latter was free to decide whether or not to ask the King to act on behalf of the Irish people.

De Valera contended that it was an appropriate time to introduce the legislation so that there could be no doubt about the new King's position, as far as the Irish people were concerned, from the very moment of his accession to the throne. The President stressed that the new legislation was not really changing anything; it was only clarifying what had been 'the fundamental positon in practice.' The connection with the Crown was being maintained, he said, for 'the only functions which in fact the King exercises.'[44]

'We are clearing up the political constitutional situation,' de Valera explained to the Dáil. 'We are making clear to everyone what the situation is, and we are removing fictions. Whatever justification there might be in British history or British constitutional theory for such fiction, there is no justification in our case. It is very much better that our people should see clearly, with no fog and no mist of constitutional theory about it.'

Britain was suddenly faced with a *fait accompli* while she was in the midst of a serious constitutional crisis. The cabinet committee on Irish affairs held an urgent meeting on 15 December 1936 in order to consider whether the External Relations Act provided the minimum 'necessary to secure membership of the Commonwealth.' By all previous reckonings, the legislation clearly did not, but the British were obviously grasping at straws. They took comfort in the fact that Article 1 of the existing Irish constitution, which declared that 'the Irish Free State is a co-equal member' of the British Commonwealth, had not been tampered with.[45] But much to their dismay, they soon learned that the new consitution was going to do away with it and also abolish the office of Governor-General, which would be replaced by an elected President.

The proposed constitution began with a neo-theocratic preamble* emphasising that it would be autochthonous. Although the word 'republic' was never used, it was a republican document. There was no mention of the King or any ties with the British Commonwealth. These

---

* In the Name of the Most Holy Trinity, from Whom is all authority and to Whom, as our final end, all actions both of men and States must be referred.

were recognised only in the External Relations Act, which would remain as ordinary legislation that could be amended at will by parliament, while the provisions of the Constitution would be ratified by popular referendum, with the result that the latter could only be amended by the people. Other significant aspects of the document, which was accepted by the people on 1 July 1937 and came into operation on 29 December 1937, were that the name of the state would henceforth be known as Ireland, or *Éire* in the Irish language. The prime minister was to be known by the Irish name *Taoiseach*, meaning chief or leader. Article 2 of the Consitution claimed sovereignty over 'the whole island of Ireland, its islands and territorial seas', but the following article declared that 'pending the reintegration of the national territory' the constitution and the laws passed by the Dublin parliament would have the same 'extent of application as the laws' of the Irish Free State.

When confronted with the constitutional proposals, MacDonald told his cabinet colleagues that it would be most difficult to throw the Twenty-six Counties out of the Commonwealth because de Valera was retaining the King for external purposes, which were after all the monarch's most important functions, seeing that the King personally discharged external functions, while a representative or deputy normally performed the internal functions within the dominions. Other cabinet members were in essential agreement, so MacDonald was authorised to recommend to the dominions that they should recognise the fundamental position of the Irish state within the British Commonwealth as unaltered by the new constitution.

The only public objection that the British made was in the form of a declaration just before the Constitution came into operation, to the effect that they recognised the new name, 'Ireland', as relating only to the area previously known as the Irish Free State, and that it did not in any way affect the position of Northern Ireland as an integral part

We, the people of Éire,
Humbly acknowledging all our obligation to our Divine Lord, Jesus Christ, Who sustained our fathers through centuries of trial, . . .
Do hereby adopt, enact and give to ourselves this Constitution.

of the United Kingdom of Great Britain and Northern Ireland.

In less than six years de Valera had unilaterally dismantled most of the disagreeable aspects of the 1921 Treaty, in spite of some determined opposition on the home front. He was convinced that the British were in touch with the Cosgraveites and that they were following a 'definite plan of campaign' to bring down his government. Moreoever he was further disturbed by the intimidating behaviour of Republican elements, especially their Bass campaign, which he described as 'damn foolacting business'. He warned that 'disaster awaits the country if the stupidity that is manifesting itself is allowed to continue.'[46]

Gradually the President found it necessary to take drastic action against his civil war colleagues. He was anxious to preserve his ties with them, but he was not prepared to allow his 'desire for unity to be used as a means of trying to blackmail us into adopting a policy which we know could only lead our people to disaster.'[47]

'We desire unity,' de Valera emphasised, 'but desires will get us nowhere unless we can get some accepted basis for determining what the national policy shall be and where leadership shall lie. What is the use of talking any more with people who are too stupid or too pigheaded to see this. A nation in its struggle can no more be successful than an army can without a plan of campaign and an accepted leadership to see it through.'[48]

During the mid 1930s the IRA was responsible for a number of deaths — the most sensational of which was the killing of Admiral Boyle Sommerville in Castletownshend in March 1936. The seventy-two-year-old retired Royal Navy Admiral was murdered for obliging young men who had sought his help in getting into the British navy.

De Valera denounced that crime and had the IRA banned shortly afterwards. 'If one section of the community could claim the right to build up a political army,' he explained, 'so could another, and it would not be long before this country would be rent asunder by rival military factions.' He added that 'if a minority tries to have its way by force against the will of the majority it is inevitable that the majority will resist by force, and this can only mean civil war.'[49]

Opponents were quick to observe that de Valera was talking in terms that were very different from 1922 when he had maintained that the minority had a right to uphold its views with arms. Although Cosgrave agreed with the suppression of the IRA, he still tried to embarrass the President by observing cynically that the latter was a recent convert to democracy. Whether de Valera saw the incongruity of his own words may be open to question, but there can be little doubt that he thought the Treatyites had been primarily responsible for the civil war. In fact, he was so convinced that he challenged Cosgrave to agree to establishing a historical commission to look into the whole matter.

The President proposed that Cosgrave and himself should each nominate three people such as a judge, a constitutional lawyer, a professor, or a recognised student of history to serve on the commission and to ask the Roman Catholic hierarchy to nominate a bishop to act as an impartial chairman. Each side would then make all its documents available to the Commission. Cosgrave's blunt rejection of the challenge could only have further strengthened de Valera's conviction in the propriety of his own actions in 1922.

The Fianna Fáil leader was skilfully steering a middle course between his former colleagues and his civil war opponents. In 1937, for example, he annoyed the latter by refusing to attend the coronation of King George VI or the ensuing Commonwealth Conference, and he infuriated Republicans by banning a demonstration which was planned for Dublin on coronation day. When IRA leaders ignored that ban, there were violent clashes with the police. As a result some prominent Republicans, like General Tom Barry, were injured and ended up in hospital.

The Republican discontent was a constant reminder that some major issues in Anglo-Irish relations still remained to be settled. These included the ending of partition, the return of the Treaty ports, the settling of the land annuities controversy and the ending of the economic war.

CHAPTER TWO

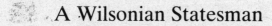

A Wilsonian Statesman

The Road to Neutrality

De Valera's unilateral implementation of what amounted to External Association went a long way towards demonstrating to the Irish people that they had achieved political freedom, while his policies at the League of Nations did much to dispel the impression — created abroad by the imposition of dominion symbolism — that the Irish Free State was not really a free agent in the area of foreign policy. Of course, the Cosgrave government had already tried to dispel that notion both by viewing matters that came up in Geneva 'from the aspect of narrow nationalism' and by seeking and eventually securing a three year seat on the Council of the League.[1] But it was de Valera who was afforded the real opportunities of using the seat to demonstrate Irish independence to the rest of the world.

As his own Minister for External Affairs, he frequently attended sessions of the League, where he used the Council seat which his government inherited, and the major international crises that all too regularly propelled the League's activities into the forefront of world affairs during the 1930s, to take stands on issues that afforded him a great deal of scope for making an international impression. It would be wrong to suggest that he cynically used those crises for selfish motives. He did not. In fact, he won quite a reputation for himself as a statesman by courageously taking up positions that were sometimes unpopular with the usually indifferent and often ill-informed electorate at home in Ireland. He advocated policies that were primarily aimed at strengthening the League so that it could be an effective force for justice in the world. Those actions are of interest to this study not only because of their significance in demonstrating Irish independence in international affairs but also because the reputation that de Valera won at the League of Nations helped him to overcome the strains that had developed in Anglo-Irish relations during the period. Moreover, what happened then played no small part in his decision to remain neutral during the Second World War, which was the action that finally dispelled the notion abroad that Ireland was politically subservient to Britain.

Nineteen-thirty-two, the year that de Valera came to power, was a particularly critical year for the League of Nations. The Japanese had been flouting the Covenant with their invasion of Manchuria, which this was the first real trial of the League's ability to prevent war. In addition the test had begun on the question of disarmament, which was one of the organisation's most cherished goals. Since neither the United States nor the Soviet Union were members of the League it was necessary to convene the Disarmament Conference outside the organisation, although it was nevertheless held under its auspices. The conference, which opened in February 1932, made only meagre and tortuous progress, notwithstanding the open expressions of support from every government. Things certainly were not auguring well for the League's efforts to arrange a similar Economic Conference to overcome the worldwide depression.

It was against such a backdrop that the League was due to meet in Geneva in September 1932. As it was the Irish Free State's turn to provide the President of the Council, in line with the practice of rotating the position every three months, de Valera was presented with the opportunity of an international stage for his views, but there was a lot of speculation about whether he would even bother to attend the session. He still had the reputation of being an enemy of the League, in view of his earlier criticism of the Covenant.

Nevertheless he attended the opening session of the Council on Saturday, 24 September 1932, and made a good impression by the forceful way in which he presided. He granted the Japanese a six week delay to consider the pending report of the Lytton Commission, which had been charged with investigating the Manchurian dispute, but he resolutely rebuffed their effort to secure a longer delay. Unless Japan could show some good reason, in which case he would agree to a delay of a further week, he insisted that the Council should meet to discuss the Lytton report in mid-November.

As President of the Council it also fell to de Valera to deliver the opening address to the Assembly two days later. Although the secretariat customarily drafted the speech, de Valera discarded the text prepared for him and delivered one of his own instead. When he rose to speak in the Assembly it was obvious that his reputation as an enemy of the League had preceded him, because there was no applause — the customary politeness shown to any presiding officer.

His address was one of remarkable simplicity and common sense that spotlighted the League's shortcomings, and emphasised the need to strengthen the organisation in order to provide it with the influence needed to achieve its goals. He began by referring to the overall international situation in which the various labour, health and communications organisations of the League had successsfully promoted international co-operation. 'But,' he added, 'I do not think I shall be accused of exaggeration if I say that the measure of progress which has so far been made falls far short of what I am convinced are the desires and expectations of the people of the world.'[2]

Those desires and expectations were important because the League needed the support of world opinion. 'Out beyond the walls of this Assembly,' he explained, 'there is the public opinion of the world, and if the League is to prosper, or even survive, it must retain the support and confidence of that public opinion as a whole.' In the last analysis, he believed that the League had 'no sanctions but the force of world opinion.' Consequently the organisation was going through an extremely trying period because the eyes of the world were trained on it to see if it could overcome its existing difficulties.

'Let us be frank with ourselves,' de Valera said. 'There is on all sides complaint, criticism and suspicion. People are complaining that the League is devoting its activity to matters of secondary or very minor importance, while the vital international problems of the day, problems which touch the very existence of our peoples, are being shelved or postponed or ignored.' Charges were being levelled against the international body not only in the belief that the money spent on it was being wasted, seeing that the various conferences were coming up with 'apparently meagre, face-saving results', but also on the grounds that small nations were being denied the equality of influence to which they were entitled under the Covenant. Indeed there was criticism, he said, that little more than lip-service was being paid to the principles of the Covenant, because influential national interests seemed capable of paralysing the actions of the League, with the more powerful among them being able to smite the organisation with apparent 'impunity'.

While those in the Assembly could feel satisfied with some of the accomplishments of the organisation, he warned that such satisfaction was not universally shared by people outside. Many uninformed and unjustified charges had been made. 'We are defendants at the bar of public opinion,' he said, 'with a burden of justification upon us which is almost overwhelming.'

The one effective way of silencing the criticism, de Valera added, was to enlist the support of millions of apathetic people by showing that the Covenant was indeed 'a solemn pact, the obligations of which no State, great or small, will find it possible to ignore.' All countries needed to adhere to the principles of the Covenant, or else there would inevitably be an arms race as governments sought to protect their own national rights. He therefore advocated that 'no State should be permitted to jeopardise the common interest by selfish action, contrary to the Covenant, and no State is powerful enough to stand for long against the League if the governments of the League and their peoples are determined that the Covenant shall be upheld.'

The speech was a statesmanlike one in which de Valera

concentrated on broad international problems and resisted any temptation to use the occasion as a forum for airing his own government's economic and political grievances against Britain. In fact, his only reference to Ireland was to stress that the Irish people wished to live 'in peace with their neighbours and with the world.'

When he finished the Assembly seemed dumbfounded. According to the *Irish Times,* he sat down to 'a stony silence, unbroken by a single note of applause.' The newspaper itself welcomed the speech. 'We cannot be surprised,' it declared in its editorial column, 'that Geneva received this unwelcome homily in silence; but, for once at least, the world will be inclined to applaud Mr de Valera.'[3]

The *Daily Express* of London, which headlined its story, 'Geneva Stunned by de Valera Onslaught', also reported that the speech was received in silence, as did the more staid *Manchester Guardian*, and the *New York Herald Tribune,* which reported that 'not a hand was raised in applause.' Those newspapers gave the unmistakable impression that the delegates from the various countires resented the speech, but according to Joseph Connolly, who was a member of the Irish delegation, that impression was wrong, because Geneva had actually welcomed the address. He recalled that while there had indeed been a stunned silence at the end of the speech, it was followed by a burst of genuine applause.[4]

'It was the most candid piece of criticism that within my recollection any League chairman has ever dared to utter,' the correspondent of the London *News Chronicle* reported. 'Yet the speech was moderate in tone, entirely without bitterness, and, indeed, indicative of the speaker's sympathy with the work and aims of the League.' This report added that afterwards 'in the lobbies the speech received nothing but praise.' The correspondent of the London *Daily Herald* was equally impressed. 'Mr de Valera this morning made the best speech I ever heard from a President of the League,' he reported. 'That is not only my own judgment. It is the opinion of almost every League journalist with whom I have spoken.'

The speech was well received internationally. 'It caused

something of a sensation at the time and received great publicity all over the world,' recalled Connolly. Indeed the remarks were given very prominent coverage in the United States, where the *New York Times* devoted an extensive report and also a favourable editorial to the address. 'Rarely had Geneva heard such a speech,' the newspaper reported on its front page. 'It was Mr de Valera's personal work, and together with the way he presided over the Council Saturday it unquestionably made him the outstanding personality of this session.'

Connolly was surprised that the address had such an impact. Although it was a good speech, he noted that 'it contained nothing save what any honest, intelligent observer of world affairs would have been bound to express at the time.' He therefore concluded that the novelty must have been its basic frankness.

'It was the simple blunt truth that made the speech something of a sensation,' he wrote. 'Geneva and the League were not accustomed to that type of speech.'[5]

The Montreal *Star* observed that the address 'revealed with brutal frankness the seriousness of the situation confronting the League. It gave the delegates practically nothing to cheer about but plenty to ponder over.' At the same time the *Manchester Guardian* declared that 'the weight of world opinion' was behind de Valera's criticism, and it noted that if he had done anything to apprise the leaders of the great powers of that fact, he could 'return to Ireland feeling that he has done a good day's work.'

Although *The Times* of London also devoted a favourable editorial to the speech, it nevertheless went on to observe that the Irish leader should have gone on to enumerate the League's successes. Some people actually interpreted his remarks as destructive criticism of the League. Observing that there was 'a touch of rather bitter irony in the spectacle of Mr de Valera, of all people in the world,' delivering such an address, the *New York Herald-Tribune* noted in an editorial that he was himself a flaming embodiment of that excessive nationalism which more than any single force has been responsible for the League's present state.'[6] While de Valera was again being depicted as an enemy of the League, he took the opportunity of explaining his views on Radio Nations, the League's radio station, on 2 October 1932.

'I spoke not as an enemy of the League,' he declared, 'but as one who wishes the League to be strengthened and developed as the best visible means of securing peace among the nations, and of solving the major political and economic problems which face the world today.'[7] He had, he explained, simply repeated criticism that was being widely made and shared by most people in Ireland, but he did not necessarily believe in all of it himself. Some of the allegations were obviously unfounded and did not stand up when confronted with the League's achievements. Yet there were other charges that could not be dismissed, and these faults needed to be corrected if the League were to achieve its worthy aims.

De Valera believed that the organisation should be strengthened in a number of ways. First of all it needed to demonstrate that if it could not actually prevent international aggression, it would at least be able to bring sufficient pressure to bear on contending parties to terminate hostilities and then arrange for a just settlement by arbitration. Secondly, he was anxious that the League should broaden its base by the inclusion of those countries — especially the major powers — that were not members. And thirdly, he wanted the organisation reformed so that it could deal with problems before they reached a crisis point, or actual hostilities. He therefore suggested that the League's structure should be made sufficiently supple to take account of changing conditions. His commitment to those principles was repeatedly demonstrated in the next few years both by his outspoken support of the Covenant and by his willingness to take stands that were politically courageous as far as the Irish scene was concerned.

Although de Valera had judiciously avoided mentioning Japan by name in his address to the Assembly, there could be little doubt that he was alluding to her when he talked about the necessity of ensuring that any aggressor should not profit from aggression. During November when he presided over the Council's deliberations on the Lytton

Commission's report he resolutely resisted the efforts of the Japanese delegation to undermine the report, which was basically very critical of Japan's role in Manchuria. The commission had concluded not only that Japan had not undertaken the venture in self-defence, as Tokyo had asserted, but also that the so-called independent state of Manchukuo, established in Manchuria, was a mere Japanese puppet from which Japanese troops had not even been withdrawn.

Although confronted with obstructionist tactics by the Japanese representative, with whom he frequently clashed, de Valera was not intimidated. He won the admiration of the *New York Times* correspondent for not only being 'an effective presiding officer' but also for instilling an 'energetic tone' into the proceedings.[8] When the Japanese delegate argued that the commission's work was finished once it presented its report, de Valera ruled otherwise and, over vociferous Japanese objections, insisted upon giving the commission an opportunity of replying to the comments made about the report by both the Japanese and Chinese representatives.

In spite of the delaying tactics of the Japanese, the President quickly managed to get the report referred to the Assembly, with the warning that 'it would be an intolerable defiance of public opinion,' if the League's machinery were not used to end the dispute. He was particuarly critical of the attitude of the Japanese delegation which he condemned for not having 'accepted the principles of settlement suggested by the commission,' but he also attached some blame to the Chinese delegation for taking a rather equivocal stand, seeing that it 'stated its desire to reserve the right to present its observations on the conditions of settlement at a later date.'[9]

When the Assembly convened on 6 December 1932 Joseph Connolly represented the Irish Free State, and assumed a forceful role. Together with the representatives of Czechoslovakia, Spain and Sweden, he submitted a resolution calling on the League to take action 'with a view to ensuring a settlement of the dispute on the basis' of the Lytton commission's recommendations. He was not deterred by the realisation that the resolution would offend Japan, and he warned other representatives that they could not afford to shrink from their responsibilities under the Covenant. 'If the League falters or hesitates, fearing lest by its action it may offend,' Connolly declared, 'then it will not survive and will not deserve to survive.'[10]

Notwithstanding the hardline assumed by 'the small four', as they were dubbed, the big powers took a vacillating stand. The French representative adopted a timid approach, though he did go on to imply that France would carry out her obligations under the Covenant, if no solution could otherwise be found. But Sir John Simon, the British representative, 'implied the opposite if anything'. His statement was generally adjudged the weakest of all. While he cited the Lytton report several times, Simon invariably confined himself to passages critical of China and repeatedly stressed the difficulties of the situation, or the need to be 'practical'. The speech had a disastrous effect on whatever chance there was of the League taking a strong stand.[11]

Connolly was bitter afterwards. When Simon congratulated him on his speech, the Irish representative was far from placated. If the Englishman was hoping for a reciprocal commendation, he must have been sorely disappointed.

'Well,' said Connolly, 'I don't suppose it matters much what a small country like Ireland thinks or does but for what it is worth, my opinion is that the League is now dead and that your speech and that of the French delegate have about finished it.'[12]

Britain actually sided with Italy and Germany in arguing that the hardline approach advocated by the small four would probably prevent reconciliation by offending Japan. Consequently the problem was merely turned over to a committee of the League for its suggestions. Thus the energetic approach taken by de Valera within the Council and the strong stand adopted by his government in the Assembly all went for naught, because although the Assembly did eventually adopt the Lytton report, its temporising had virtually killed any chance of decisive action, and Japan simply thumbed her nose at the international body by withdrawing from it in protest.

Being of the opinion that the League had been weakened from its inception by the exclusion of some powers, de Valera undoubtedly regretted the withdrawal of Japan, as it unquestionably weakened further the moral authority of the organisation. But there appeared a chance to repair some of that damage when there were reports that the Soviet Union was anxious to join the League in 1934. De Valera therefore supported Soviet admission although it left him open to the renewed charge at home of being a communist sympathiser. 'It is obvious,' he told the Assembly on 12 September 1934, 'that anyone who has the interest of the League at heart, and looks upon the League as an instrument for the preservation of world peace, must desire to see in the League a nation of the importance of Russia.'[13]

But the Irish leader was not prepared to support Soviet entry at any price. At the time there was a problem because the Soviets did not want to apply formally, and thereby take the chance of being refused entry, unless they first had an assurance that their request would not be rejected. The Assembly had comparatively recently established a precedent by inviting Mexico and Turkey to join the League, so Moscow was therefore entitled to expect similar treatment. But the resolutions in the other two cases had been passed by the unanimous consent of the Assembly, and this could not be done in the case of the Soviet Union, as there were objections to issuing an invitation. The League could not therefore invite the Soviet Union to join, unless the latter first applied for membership — at which time the request would only need the support of a two-thirds majority of the Assembly.

Some member states planned to draw up a petition in which two-thirds of the members would not only invite the Soviet Union to join the League, but would pledge their support and thus ensure her acceptance into the organisation. But these tactics would mean that the traditional right of a country to have its objections heard before a decision was made would be circumvented. De Valera therefore opposed the manoeuvre. He argued that the question should be brought openly bèfore the Assembly so that the minority opposed to Soviet membership could have their say. This would then eliminate the suspicion of intrigue that could be damaging to the League.

In the course of his speech de Valera made it clear that he favoured Soviet membership although the political and religious ideals of the Soviet Union and the Irish Free State were poles apart. Afterwards when a Swiss representative voiced misgivings on behalf of millions of Christians over the question of Soviet membership, he was taken to task by the French Foreign Minister, Jean Louis Barthou, who contended that the admittance of the Soviet Union was simply a political question. De Valera, in turn, criticised the attitude of the Frenchman.

'It is not sufficient to say that we are here concerned merely with politics,' he said. 'No politics that are in any sense real can exclude considerations of the purpose of human life and the end which men's existence is designed to serve.'[14] He added that unless the Soviets were prepared to give guarantees of religious freedom, their entry into the League would not really contribute towards peace. He therefore took the opportunity of calling on the communist regime to accord religious liberty to its own people by extending the guarantees given to the United States the previous year when, on securing offical American recognition, the Moscow government guaranteed religious freedom to Americans in the Soviet Union.

The impasse over Soviet membership was eventually settled by referring the question to a committee, where the various members could voice their objections. Then thirty-four countries signed a petition inviting the Soviet Union to apply for membership, and Moscow gladly complied.

No doubt de Valera's remarks concerning the need for religious liberties in the Soviet Union helped to mollify the opposition which he could expect at home for supporting communists, but it would be wrong to suggest that he did not believe sincerely in what he was advocating. A few days later he also spoke out on another aspect of human rights, or to be more specific, the problems of minority rights that were soon to become the pretext for not only a series of major crises in Europe but for the outbreak of war in 1939.

When the Polish delegation advocated that a uniform code for the protection of minority rights should be drawn up, for example, de Valera supported the idea and stressed that the League had a responsibility in the matter on account of the actions of those who had framed the Versailles Treaty, because they had contributed to the problem. 'President Wilson,' he said, 'used to protest against the cynical "handing over of peoples from sovereignty to sovereignty as though they were chattels", and when we were looking at the treaties that were being worked out at Versailles, some of us, at any rate, could not help thinking that the protest had been completely lost sight of when the war was over.' The major powers had arbitrarily handed over minorities at Versailles, with the result that the League of Nations had a duty to defend the rights of those people.[15]

'I suggest,' de Valera added, 'we could begin by a convention to universalise those sacred rights of *the individual* which should not be taken from him under any pretext by any majority whatever.' He proposed that a committee should be established to 'obtained agreement on a universal measure of protection for minorities against unfair discrimination anywhere.'

In this speech the Irish leader could not resist making reference to the situation in Ireland, where he said, 'An artificial area was cut off, and all along its boundary there are majorities adjacent to the main part who belong to it in race, religion, language and everything else.' The interjection was brief and to the point.

'The ideal solution to the minority problems,' he said, immediately returning to the question in general, 'would be to transfer, where possible, the minority back to its original home; but if that cannot be done, the pratical solution would be to give to the minority, if it is homogenous and inhabiting a continuous area, the greatest amount of local autonomy that can be consistent with the maintenance of the unity of the state.' Recognising that there would undoubtedly be difficulties, he advocated that these should be examined immediately, instead of waiting until some country like Poland precipitated a crisis. 'The position should be thoroughly investigated and a report prepared,' he said. That report would deal both with individual rights that could be guaranteed universally and with 'those particular minority problems that have arisen out of the war.'

During the same session of the League the Irish President also spoke out forcefully on the war that had been going on since 1932 between Bolivia and Paraguay over possession of the almost desolate area known as the Chaco. As President of the Council in 1932 he had suggested that the League should intervene to stop the Chaco war. But his efforts to involve the organisätion were frustrated by authorities in the United States, whose jealous attachment to the Monroe Doctrine, led them to advocate that the League should stand aside and allow a commission comprising of representatives from a number of American republics to try to settle the conflict. Both of the contending nations supported the suggestion, so the League had little choice but to stand aside. Nevertheless the various efforts of the American countries acting separately and in conjunction with one another were unsuccessful. Initially the Bolivians were the principal culprits in frustrating peace efforts, at least while they thought that they were winning the war.

When the American states abandoned their peace efforts in frustration, the League decided to establish a commission to investigate the dispute and recommend ways of ending hostilities. Both Paraguay and Bolivia agreed to the idea, but as the commission was about to start its investigation in July 1933, the two belligerents requested a postponement until their neighbouring countries could again try to secure a settlement. This led to a further delay of some months before their neighbours formally refused to become involved.

By the time the commission began its deliberations the war had begun to swing back in favour of Paraguay, whose government then flatly rejected the commission's peace proposals. Frustrated, the commission returned to Geneva and recommended that the only practical method of ending hostilities was to place an embargo on the export of munitions to the countries involved. After some initial difficulties, an embargo was enforced and was virtually complete in August 1934.

Bolivia appealed to the League to deal with the Chaco question the following month. And in the ensuing discussion de Valera — who had been elected chairman of the organisation's Sixth Committee, which dealt with political questions — was strongly critical that things had been allowed to drag on for so long. He complained of the repeated involvment of outside agencies. 'There should,' he said, 'no longer be a doorway through which the parties can leave one procedure for another and experiment with a fresh formula when the negotiations take a turn unsatisfactory to them.'[16]

De Valera believed that it was time for the League to play its prescribed role by enforcing the procedure laid down in the Covenant. A committee should be established, he said, and given two months to bring about conciliation. If it failed to do so within the specified time, the Assembly should consider the case and pronounce its judgement. While he believed that the territorial dispute should be left to the arbitration of the Court of International Justice, he went on to make what the *New York Times* described as the 'sensational suggestion' that the League should establish its own peace-keeping force to keep the belligerents apart.[17]

'It seems to me that this dispute can be brought to an end quickly,' de Valera declared, 'if we are determined to act up fully to our responsibility.' He was not simply looking for an end to hostilities without regard to the principles involved. 'I would not like either of the contending nations to think that we are concerned only with stopping the warfare somehow and not concerned with the just determination of the dispute,' he emphasised. 'Everyone of us desire, not merely that the dispute should end, but that justice should be done.'

Actually it was not necessary for the League to take further action. The arms embargo proved very effective, and, as the two countries were exhausted not only militarily and financially, but also in terms of morale, the war simply ground to a halt.

Following the League's limited success in the Chaco war, the Irish leader was obviously hopeful that the organisation might play an effective role in preventing Italian aggression against Ethiopia in the autumn of 1935. From the outset he looked on the Ethiopian crisis as a crucial test for the League. Even before leaving for Geneva in September 1935 he announced that his own government's attitude was going to be 'determined by its desire to see the League of Nations preserved as an effective guarantee of peace.' Consequently he said that he would 'be in full sympathy with any effort' to avert hostilities in Abyssinia.[18]

While in Geneva de Valera made it clear that he thought the League of Nations should be thoroughly reformed so that it could make binding decisions which even the major powers would be unable to ignore. As things stood, he explained in an address broadcast to the United States over Radio Nations, people throughout the world had not been prepared to forego the opportunity of satisfying their own selfish ambitions at the expense of others. 'Theoretically, and in the abstract,' he said, 'they assent and subscribe to the principle that the rule of law should be substituted for that of force. But, in practice, each nation wants to reserve to itself the right to interpret the law, to be a judge in its own case, and, if its interest should require it, to defy and disobey.'[19]

The various alliances, treaties and non-aggression pacts made by members of the League showed how little confidence the countries involved had in the Covenant as a guarantee of security. 'Each distrusts the professed good faith of its neighbour and rival, and those who depend upon the League and the Covenant for their security find themselves in danger of being taken unawares because of their confidence,' he said. As a result he felt that the League was 'in imminent peril'.

It was not going to survive, de Valera warned, 'unless certain basic principles are accepted and all reservations in regard to them set aside.' In particular, he emphasised that the theory of absolute national sovereignty should be abandoned and the unanimity rule of the League changed. In addition, the organisation's structure needed to be less rigid so that wrongs within the existing state system could be redressed.

'Only what is fundamentally just has a right to last,' the Irish leader declared. 'The rights of the haves and have-nots need to be adjusted from time to time in the case of States as of individuals within the state, and when a wrong cries out for redress or an evil for a cure, there must be some means of providing them in time without waiting for a threat of war to compel attention.' He therefore suggested that there should 'be some tribunal by which the law shall be interpreted and applied, and, finally, there must be some means by which its judgments can be enforced against a state which might think it to its advantage to ignore them.'

As it was, the League fell far short of the kind of organisation that de Valera desired, but it was nevertheless a real effort 'to order international affairs by reason and justice instead of by force.' Suspicion over the motives of the League's founders should not deter people from supporting the organisation, he said, because the alternative as far as Europe was concerned was 'a return to the law of the jungle'. He went on to advocate that the efforts of all right-thinking people should be directed towards improving the League so that it could quickly develop into the ideal model envisioned. 'To destroy it now would be a crime against humanity,' he concluded. 'To maintain it we must live up to its obligations.'

In the following days de Valera showed that he was personally prepared to live up to those obligations and provide what support he could muster to give his proposals teeth. 'The final test of the League and all that it stands for has come,' he told the Assembly on 16 September 1935. 'Our conduct in this crisis will determine whether it is better to let it lapse and disappear and be forgotten. Make no mistake, if on any pretext whatever we were to permit the sovereignty of even the weakest state amongst us to be unjustly taken away, the whole foundation of the League would crumble into dust. If the pledge of security is not universal, if it is not to apply to all impartially, if there be pick-

ing and choosing and jockeying and favouritism, if one
aggressor is to be given a free hand while another is
restrained, then it is far better that the old system of
alliances should return and that each nation should do what
it can to prepare for its own defence. Without universality,
the League can only be a snare. If the Covenant is not
observed as a whole for all and by all, then there is no
Covenant.'[20]

Ireland was determined to uphold her responsibilities in
the crisis. 'By our own choice and without compulsion we
entered into the obligations of the Covenant,' de Valera
emphasised. 'we shall fulfil these obligations in the letter
and in the spirit. We have given our word and we shall keep
it.'

De Valera's logic was clear and simple. People should
put the same effort into preserving peace as they would
squander on war. 'Yesterday,' he said, 'there were no
finances to give the workless the opportunity of earning
their bread; tomorrow, money unlimited will be found to
provide for the manufacture of instruments of destruction.'
Consequently he advocated that the League should be
placed on a stable foundation so that it could remove the
causes of future disputes and settle the major questions in a
spirit of friendly co-operation and justice before another
major conflict reeked havoc among the nations. In fact, he
thought that the Ethiopian crisis could be turned to the
League's advantage because it provided the necessary
impetus to weld the members of the organisation together
in 'a common purpose of self-preservation'.

The Irish leader's optimism had undoubtedly been
prompted by the firm stand which Sir Samuel Hoare, the
British Foreign Secretary, had taken against Italy's
threatened aggression. Only the previous week Hoare had
made a stirring speech to the Assembly promising that
Britain would stand resolutely 'for the collective maintenance of the Covenant in its entirety, and particularly for
steady and collective resistance to all acts of unprovoked
aggression.'[21]

The Foreign Secretary's speech was received with a tremendous outburst of international approval. People who

had for years been highly sceptical of the League's ability to function as envisaged by its founders, suddenly discovered that the organisation might after all be effective, if not in actually preventing aggression, at least in ensuring that the aggressor nation would not profit by her hostility. The support of world opinion that de Valera had said was so vital to the League in his first appearance before the Assemby three years earlier, was at last undoubtedly aligned behind the organisation.

Even though Ethiopia offered concessions to the Italians that went beyond the bounds of justice and equity, Benito Mussolini, the Italian leader, was bent on military conquest. He ignored the Ethiopian offer and his own country's obligation to respect the Covenant. On 3 October 1935 Italian troops began their invasion of Ethiopia.

Next day de Valera went on national radio to explain the situation to the Irish people. He noted that Japan's violation of the Covenant had shaken the League to its very foundations a few years earlier. 'It is obvious,' he said, 'that if a second similar successful violation takes place, the League of Nations must disappear as an effective safeguard for individual members.' Thus he felt that the League would only become a menace because it would act as 'a trap for states trusting in it, leading them to neglect adequate measures for their own defence.'[22]

People were prepared to exploit the advantages of an organisation like the League, he explained, but there was 'no such alacrity in fulfilling the corresponding obligations to bear the burdens or make the sacrifices which the common interest may demand.' Countries would use the League to adjust disputes by arbitration or other peaceful means, but it was a different matter when it came to taking part in disciplinary measures to compel some country 'to refrain from aggression or to respect his international undertakings.'

While the theory of collective security appeared quite simple and readily won acceptance, it was a totally different matter to ensure its application in practice. The chief obstacle had been the reluctance of countries 'to commit themselves irrevocably to the League or to agree in

advance to a detailed system of sanctions for the enforcement of the Covenant.' Nevertheless the President emphasised that he had 'consistently held that the obligations
of the Covenant should be enforced. That was our position
in the case of the Sino-Japanese conflict. That is our position in the present case.'

If economic sanctions proved ineffective, de Valera
explained that the Council could then recommend military
measures. But these would not be legally binding on the
Irish Free State without the consent of the Irish parliament.
Nevertheless he continued in terms that seemed to hint
strongly that he believed that such consent should be given,
if necessary.* While in Geneva the previous month he had
predicted that no system of international government could
be effective until 'the theory of the absolute states, interpreted to mean that a state is above all law, must be abandoned.'[23] Back in Dublin he made it clear that he thought
that the Covenant's concession to national sovereignty was
actually weakening the League. 'The difficulty with the
League,' he said, 'is not that the obligations it imposes are
too strict, but rather that they are not strict enough to be
effective.'[24]

'To effect the necessary changes will be an extremely
difficult task,' he explained, 'even if the League survives
the present crisis. But it is a task to which all right-minded
people, who believe that human society can be ordered
according to reason and is not doomed to remain for ever
subject to brute force and passion, will devote themselves
in confident hope of ultimate success.' Those were strong
sentiments indeed from a man with the reputation of being
an unyielding champion of national sovereignty.

'Whether or not one accepts Mr de Valera's views on
these grave issues,' a long-standing critic wrote, 'one must
realise that he has approached them sincerely and in no
petty spirit, and that he is prepared to carry his opinions to
their logical conclusions.'[25]

De Valera's unequivocal support of the League actually
met with a certain amount of criticism at home, not

* He later confirmed this, see p. 157

only from opposition benches, but also from within his own party. One Fianna Fáil deputy, Kathleen Clarke, the widow of one of the 1916 leaders, contended that the government should have used its stand at the League 'for bargaining purposes' in order to extract economic concessions from the British in return for supporting Britain's call for sanctions against Italy. But the President refuted that criticism vigorously. 'If we want justice for ourselves, we ought to stand for justice for others,' he emphasised. 'As long as I have the honour of representing any Government here outside, I stand, on every occasion, for what I think is just and right, thinking thereby I will help the cause of Ireland, and I will not bargain that for anything.'[26] On another occasion when some opposition critics expressed amusement that he was pursuing the same policy as the British, he responded with an effective rejoiner by observing that a person on the road to heaven would not turn around and go in the other direction simply because his worst enemy was taking the same road.

Frank MacDermot, who was both a founding member and a vice-president of the leading opposition party, which was then going under the transitional name of United Ireland Party, became so disgusted with the tactics of his colleagues that he resigned from the party. His action apparently had a salutary effect because when it came to the actual voting on a bill to institute sanctions against Italy, only three members of the opposition voted against the measure.

Initially sanctions seemed likely to succeed under Britain's strong leadership, especially after the British government had a resounding victory in a general election held in mid-October. Baldwin and his colleagues had campaigned on a promise to pursue the sanctions with full vigour and 'do all in our power to uphold the Covenant. If ever there was an opportunity of striking a decisive blow in a generous cause with minimum risk,' Winston Churchill wrote, 'it was here and now.'[27]

But the Baldwin government had no intention of upholding its promises in regard to Ethiopia. It was afraid that if the sanctions were enforced with full vigour, they might either provoke an armed confrontation with Mussolini, or else they might undermine him to the extent that he would be driven from power — thereby leaving a vacuum in Italy for the communists to fill. Hoare therefore assured the French Foreign Minister, Pierre Laval, that Britain had no intention of going further than economic and financial sanctions. She would not, for instance, be prepared to institute a naval blockade or even close the Suez Canal to Italian troops and supplies bound for Ethiopia. 'It is obvious,' de Valera told the Dáil afterwards, 'that, if the powers were really serious and were prepared to take definite measures, the closing of the Suez Canal would have been resorted to as one measure. Consequently, it was obvious the League of Nations was taking half-measures which could not in the ultimate fail to be ineffective.'[28] As Churchill later wrote, 'the measures pressed with so great a parade were not real sanctions to paralyse the aggressor, but merely such half-hearted sanctions as the aggressor would tolerate.' He added sarcastically that the League 'proceeded to the rescue of Abyssinia on the basis that nothing must be done to hamper the invading Italian armies.'[29]

The British position was exposed in December 1935 with the publication of an agreement that Hoare had reached with Laval to press for a compromise solution whereby Ethiopia would be forced to cede territory to the Italians. Although the notorious Hoare-Laval Pact was scrapped in the face of bitter public criticism in Britain, it — together with the unwillingness to adopt effective sanctions — dealt what would prove to be a lethal blow to the League of Nations, or at any rate to de Valera's hopes that the organisation could be an effective instrument for preventing aggression.

The Irish leader quickly recognised that the sanctions had failed. Even though many of his critics had for long been contending that he always sought to make capital out of exploiting anti-British feeling, he did not try to blame either Britain or France specifically for the failure. Rather, he attributed fault to the League as a whole. He was obviously deeply disappointed. 'My view,' he told the Dáil, 'is

that there was never a better chance for the League of
Nations to be successful against a great power as there was
in this case, and that if it failed in the case of Italy it was
bound to fail in the case of other powers. As things stood,
therefore, he felt that the organisation no longer had the
'confidence of the ordinary people of the world.' And, he
stressed in the Dáil: 'It does not command our confidence.'[30]

Speaking in Geneva on 2 July 1936 he called on the
League Assembly to admit that it could 'do nothing effective' about Italy's violation of the Covenant. 'We have now
to confess publicly that we must abandon the victim to his
fate,'[31] which, he added, was 'the fulfilment of the worst
predictions of all who decried the League and said it could
not succeed.' He therefore asked if any small nation
represented in the Assembly could doubt 'the truth of the
warning that what is Ethiopia's fate today may well be its
own tomorrow, should the greed or the ambition of some
powerful neighbour prompt its destruction.'

'Unless the League can inspire confidence,' de Valera
added, 'it clearly cannot stand.' As the sanctions had been
introduced in the belief that they could be effective, which
had since proved erroneous, he therefore advocated that
the policy should be abandoned. 'Subscribing to what
proved to be a delusion is not the way to secure confidence,' he said. If confidence were to be restored, it could
'only be by rigidly restricting commitments to those we
know can be loyally carried out.' Henceforth economic or
financial sanctions could be effective only if members of
the League were 'prepared to back them up by military
measures.' And it was obvious, he said, that none of them
was prepared to do that on Ethiopia's behalf for fear that
the war would spread to Europe, which was the real danger
area.

De Valera advised the Assembly to concentrate immediately on 'the urgent task of preserving peace in
Europe and leave aside for the moment such questions as
how the Covenant should be altered,' in order to make the
League an 'effective and universal' world organisation. If
the great powers on whom European peace was dependent

would 'meet now in that Peace Conference which will have to be held after Europe has once more been drenched in blood' and if they would make 'in advance only a tithe of the sacrifice each of them will have to make should the war begin, the terrible menace which threatens us all today could be warded off.'

Time was running out for them, he warned, if they were to have any chance of being successful. 'The problems that distract Europe should not be abandoned to the soldiers to decide,' he asserted. 'They should be tackled now by the statesmen. If these problems cannot be settled by conciliation, let them be submitted to arbitration.' They should make the territorial and other adjustments needed 'to remove obvious causes of the war that is now threatening.'

Though there was much idealism in the address, it was the speech of a realist. The Irish leader knew that there was really little that either he or his country could do to prevent a major war. He could call on world leaders to adopt sensible policies — and indeed he did call on them repeatedly — but once they chose to ignore him then he was powerless to do anything effective.

'Despite our judicial equality here,' he told the League Assembly, 'in matters such as European peace the small states are powerless. As I have already said, peace is dependent upon the will of great states. All the small states can do, if the statesmen of greater states fail in their duty, is resolutely to determine that they will not become the tools of any great power, and that they will resist with whatever strength they may possess every attempt to force them into a war against their will.'

The failure of the sanctions against Italy, which were lifted on 15 July 1936, persuaded de Valera that the League would not be able to prevent another major conflict. As the months passed he became even more convinced that another war was imminent. Henceforth his own attitude was to pursue a policy that would allow Ireland to remain neutral in the event of such a war, so he was careful to keep the country out of situations in which there was any danger of becoming embroiled in an armed conflict on behalf of the Covenant. As far as he was concerned the Covenant's obligations that he had so firmly supported during the Manchurian Crisis, the Chaco War, and again during the Abyssinian conflict were, in effect, a casualty of the Ethiopian debacle.

Although most of de Valera's attention in foreign policy matters during the following months was devoted to Anglo-Irish affairs, he did courageously support the non-intervention policy espoused by the League during the Spanish Civil War. But his policy ran into determined opposition at home in Ireland, where people tended to look on the Spanish conflict in the grossly oversimplified terms of a struggle between Roman Catholicism and atheistic communism. Irish emotions were running so high in favour of the Nationalist forces of General Francisco Franco that when General Eoin O'Duffy announced that he was thinking of forming an Irish Brigade to fight in Spain, some six thousand men volunteered for service within a fortnight.[32] Even within the Labour Party, sentiment was so strong at the annual conference that Conor Cruise O'Brien, a young student from Trinity College, Dublin, had to be protected from physical abuse when he courageously denounced Franco.[33]

De Valera publicly stated that he hoped that Franco's forces would be victorious, but he made it clear that this was only because he looked on them as the lesser of two evils. He viewed the struggle as basically between fascism and communism, and while he detested communism, he thought the other was only slightly better. 'Fascism, even if not equally bad, is bad,' he told the Dáil. 'It is perhaps not equally bad, but it is a desperate alternative, and I hope that this country will be saved from having those alternatives as a choice.'[34]

While de Valera believed that non-intervention was in Spain's interest, his main reason for supporting the policy was because he thought that it offered the best chance of containing the Spanish conflict. His government introduced legislation forbidding Irish citizens to leave the state for Spain without special permission, and violations were made punishable by up to two years in jail and a fine of £500.

During the debate on the legislation, over which the Dáil divided on party lines, de Valera was bitterly criticised by the opposition. Observing that Spain's Roman Catholic cardinal had declared that the struggle was between the Christ and the anti-Christ, Paddy Belton contended that by characterising the conflict as merely between the 'isms' of communism and fascism, de Valera had, in effect, called the Spanish cardinal a liar. Such emotional criticism was not confined to the lunatic fringe of the oppositon. Desmond FitzGerald, a former Minister for External Affairs in the Cosgrave government, castigated de Valera for making a speech that was 'applauded by all the Communistic, liberal, pinkish newspapers in Europe.'

'If I remember rightly,' FitzGerald added, 'he actually implied criticism of the Nazi Government in Germany and their treatment of Jews.' In so far as the Nazi treatment of Jewish people was unjust FitzGerald approved of what de Valera had said, but he was nevertheless still critical that the President had made any remarks that could find favour with the 'pink liberals and Communists', who were the opponents of the Nazis.[35]

Seán Lester, the Irish diplomat who had some years earlier joined the League secretariat, was critical of the attitude that the opposition had adpoted towards de Valera's foreign policy. 'They have tried to rally all our abysmal ignorance of foreign affairs against him.'[36]

The Irish leader was really in an unenviable position. He had become so disillusioned with the League of Nations that he actually considered withdrawing the Irish Free State from the organisation in May 1937 but decided against such a move because he felt that the League at least served the function as a place of debate where leaders could discuss international problems.[37] Nevertheless he made it patently clear in the following months that he no longer felt bound by the Covenant's obligations. Henceforth, he was prepared to follow the League's lead only in instances where he agreed with that lead himself.

This became particularly evident when there were moves to reconsider the non-intervention policy adopted by most members of the League towards the Spanish conflict. That policy had been causing concern because it was preventing the democratic countries — most of whom sympathised with the Republican forces in Spain — from rendering help, although both Italy and Germany, each of whom had withdrawn from the League, were providing extensive support in the form of troops and supplies to Franco's side. Thus the League's policy had the negative effect of actually favouring Franco. When the organisation met to discuss the situation in September 1937, therefore, the Assembly considered a resolution that would appeal for the observance of non-intervention but would at the same time stipulate that the policy would be abandoned if the countries ignoring it did not comply within the near future.

Being primarily concerned with preventing the spread of the conflict, de Valera objected to the resolution for fear that it would lead to a widening of the war. He told the Assembly on 2 October 1937 that he sympathised with the sentiments calling on all countries to observe non-intervention but he considered it 'unwise that the appeal should be prejudiced by being coupled with a statement capable of being construed into a threat.' He was afraid that if others intervened, it would lead 'to a fatal competiton which could only result in a general European disaster.' Since the resolution implied counter-intervention in the event that Germany and Italy did not withdraw their forces, de Valera decided not to support the resolution. By taking his stand he wanted 'to make it clear beyond any possibility of misunderstanding that our government is not being committed to any policy or action which might result from the termination of the Non-Intervention Agreement.'[38]

The most dramatic instance of de Valera's repudiation of the obligations of the Covenant occurred in December 1937 when he announced to the Dáil that the country was opening diplomatic relations with Italy. As the new Irish Minister would be accredited to the Court of Victor Emmanuel III, in his capacity as King of Italy and *Emperor of Ethiopia,* it meant that the Dublin government would be formally recognising Italy's annexation of Ethiopia in blatant disregard for a League resolution adopted during the Manchurian crisis which bound League members 'not to recognise any situation' that had been 'brought about by means contrary to the Covenant'.

'There is a *de facto* position staring us in the face,' de Valera told the Dáil, 'and we must take account of that. If we wish to have a representative in Italy as has been our wish, then we give to the sovereign of that country the title which he has taken or which his own people have taken.' The Irish leader made it clear that he was not approving of what Italy had done, but only recognising a reality.[39]

The move actually had an enormous significance as a gesture of Irish diplomatic freedom. By signing the new minister's letter of accreditation, King George VI had given further demonstration of Irish independence, not just domestically but now also in the field of international relations. Britain had been refusing to recognise Italy's annexation of Ethiopia, so the appointment of an Irish Minister to Rome and having his credentials signed by the King, demonstrated that the British Crown was in effect divisible.

The eminent Canadian statesman, Ernest Lapointe, contended that when taken to its logical conclusion, the whole episode proved that dominions had a right to remain neutral while Britain was at war. Of course, the right of neutrality had long ago been informally recognised by British leaders, but it had been assumed that in order to exercise that right the dominion wishing to remain neutral would have to withdraw from the British Commonwealth. Lapointe felt, however, that the latest Irish action demonstrated that withdrawal would not be necessary.[40]

CHAPTER THREE

Preparing for Neutrality

Regaining the Ports

Faced with the League's obvious inability to function effectively in the area of collective security following the failure of the sanctions against Italy, de Valera had to decide what to do in the likely event of another major war. He had already made it clear that he believed that small nations should avoid such conflicts, if at all possible, but he was distinctly pessimistic about his country's chances of remaining neutral. This was because of the defence provisions of the 1921 Treaty which granted Britain naval facilities in the three Irish ports of Cobh, Berehaven, and Lough Swilly, together with rights to any other facilities she might require 'in time of war or of strained relations with a foreign power.'

The defence clauses were really the only provisions of the Treaty left to which he had taken exception in 1921 and which he had not since been able unilaterally to dismantle. As the danger of a major war increased, these took on added significance because they would effectively deny the Irish people their constitutional right to remain neutral if Britain were involved. As long as the British retained the ports, the President explained to the Dáil, the country would be liable 'to attack by any enemy of Great Britain'.[1] What he did not say then, but did admit afterwards was that he was even more worried about Britain's rights to any other facilities she might require. That stipulation posed a real dilemma.

To refuse requested facilities in wartime might lead to hostilities with Britain, while handing them over would not only incur the wrath of Britain's enemy but would also antagonise certain Irish people. De Valera explained that he was convinced that any government that handed over facilities to the British would forfeit the support of the majority of the Irish people, who would not tolerate such co-operation with Britain while partition continued.[2]

The Northern Ireland question was really one of de Valera's prime concerns. The threat of partition that had supposedly first prompted him to become involved in politics more that twenty years earlier. Since coming to power he had frequently decried Ireland's dismemberment, but he tended to put more emphasis on other problems in his speeches. It was no doubt significant that in his address to the United States after Fianna Fáil's election success of 1932 he only mentioned the issue having first dealt with the questions of unemployment, the oath, and land annuities. He did nevertheless contend that partition was the greatest wrong that Britain had done to Ireland, and he denounced, as cynical, British attempts to justify their action in the name of democracy or minority rights. 'The area cut off,' he said, 'was not determined on any principle of right or justice.'[3]

De Valera did have a point. The Six Counties were not a historic area. The British had not only partitioned Ireland but had also partitioned Ulster, with those six counties being chosen as the largest area which the predominantly Protestant unionists would be able to hold with a safe majority. That was done in blatant disregard for the fact that two of those counties actually had nationalist majorities, as had most of the areas that were contiguous to the Twenty-six Counties. And on the issue of minority rights, he noted that 'the nationalist minority in the area cut off is relatively greater than the unionist minority in the island as a whole.'[4]

During the early years of the Fianna Fáil government the President tended to put less emphasis on the partition question in his speeches at home than in those addressed to Americans. In February 1933, for example, he used the occasion of Abraham Lincoln's birthdate to denounce partition in an address to the United States.

Over the years American correspondents — to whom de Valera was usually accessible — frequently mentioned the large bust of Lincoln that the Irish leader kept in his office.

But then, that American President was an appropriate model for de Valera, who often reminded Americans that their former President had not fought the civil war to abolish slavery, but to preserve the union of the United States. 'My paramount objective is to save the Union, and not either to save or destroy slavery,' de Valera quoted Lincoln as saying. 'If I could save the Union without freeing any slave I would do it.'[5]

'The erection of this six-county area into a petty State, under the ultimate control of the British Treasury,' de Valera told the Americans, 'was a purely arbitrary act, inspired solely by considerations of British Imperial policy, and contrary to every interest of the Irish people. Imposed by force and maintained by subsidies, partition is the worst of all the many crimes committed by British statesmen against the Irish people during the last 750 years.'

The reference to Lincoln and the American civil war followed by such a denouncement of partition could have led to intense speculation about de Valera's intentions regarding Northern Ireland, had it not been for his more moderate approach to the issue at home. Barely a fortnight later, for instance, he told the Dáil that 'the only policy' that was practical for ending partition was for the Twenty-six Counties to develop in such a way as to make 'the people in the other part of Ireland wish to belong to this part.'[6] Hence economic development was a major aspect of Fianna Fáil's programme.

While de Valera had tried to avoid the economic war with Britain, he did welcome the opportunity that it afforded his government to appeal to the nationalistic instincts of the Irish people to remodel their economic system. He warned the Fianna Fáil Árd Fheis on 8 November 1932 that 'if the British Government should succeed in beating us in this fight, then you would have no freedom, because at every step they could threaten you again and force you again to obey the British. What is involved is whether the Irish nation is going to be free or not.' He wanted the economic system strong and viable enough to stand independently of Britain. He knew that some people would have to endure hardships but, as he told the Senate at the outset of the struggle, the suffering would be compensated 'by the foundation here of the sort of economic life that every Irishman who thought nationally in the past has hoped for.'[7]

Rallies were held throughout the country to encourage the people to buy Irish goods and farmers to diversify so that imports could be cut back. 'We are all brothers in this,' the President told a gathering in College Green, Dublin, 'none of us can suffer for any length of time without that suffering reflecting on the rest of us. It is our duty to stand together.'[8]

As part of its campaign, Fianna Fáil introduced a programme of industrialisation. Although many people supported the policy for purely economic reasons, it was probable that de Valera — whose interest in economic matters was limited — was primarily motivated by political considerations. It was an important status symbol in the modern world for a country to produce her own goods and be self-sufficient.[9]

From a purely political standpoint Fianna Fáil's economic policy was a success, because the government could point to some significant statistical advances, such as the fall in annual shoe imports from over five million pairs in 1931 to a low of a quarter of a million pairs in 1938, or the drop in the value of clothing imports from £5.3 millions in 1931 to less than £1 million in 1937. Britain was being significantly hurt by Irish policies in that her share of the Irish import market declined from eighty-one per cent in 1931 to fifty per cent in 1937. But those successes had been gained at a price, seeing that the govenment's political success was not matched in economic terms. The value of Irish exports to Britain dropped by more that fifty per cent between 1931 and 1938, and the Irish trade deficit reached a record £20.7 millions in 1937. Attempts to find new international markets were also a dismal failure seeing that only five per cent of Irish exports were redirected from Britain, which meant that a staggering ninety-one per cent were still going there. Moreover Britain was able to make up the disputed annuity payments with her duties on Irish imports. In fact, the British were really getting their money indirectly from the

Dublin government, which was providing export subsidies to mitigate the effects of the British duties.[10] Thus it was really in the interests of both governments that the dispute be settled.

On meeting Malcolm MacDonald in Geneva on 15 September 1937, de Valera explained that he was anxious for an amicable settlement of all outstanding issues with Britain. Although he went on to warn that it would not be possible to bring about the good relations that they would both like to see, until partition was ended, he nevertheless suggested that the two sides could at least settle the other problems in the hope that the improved Anglo-Irish relations might 'make the solution of partition itself easier.'[11]

De Valera was, of course, most interested in securing Irish unity, but MacDonald could foresee no hope of it in the near future. He explained that it was not that the British wanted partition 'for its own sake', but that they were committed to the majority in Northern Ireland.

'I asked,' de Valera recalled, 'if they would publicly state that, so far as they were concerned, they would desire partition to end.' The Dominions Secretary however was unable to promise that such a statement would be made. He simply said that a solution was going to have to wait. At that point de Valera warned him that the Dublin government 'would therefore have to consider a campaign to inform British and world opinion as to the inequity of the whole position.'

When MacDonald said that he would bring up the Anglo-Irish difficulties with his cabinet colleagues upon his return to London and would then be in touch with the President if they could put forward some proposals, de Valera suggested that as the issues were ones that would have to be decided at the highest level, it would be pointless leaving discussions to civil servants. 'I thought a delegation of British ministers could meet ours either in Dublin or in London to hammer out a settlement finally,' de Valera wrote, 'but that any such meeting would be worse than useless unless there was a reasonable prospect that a settlement could be made.'

The cabinet in Dublin endorsed the idea of discussions at

the highest level, so de Valera — who had previously let MacDonald take all the initiatives in their contacts — surprised the British on 24 November 1937 by formally suggesting the holding of ministerial talks. In his despatch to the Dominions Office, de Valera explained that the Dublin government was concerned over the deteriorating international situation and was therefore anxious to consider the country's defence posture, which 'must depend fundamentally on the relations that will exist between our two countries at the time.'[12]

The British agreed to the proposed talks, and arrangements were made for them to begin in London in the new year. MacDonald hoped that the Irish initiative might be an indication that de Valera would be 'in a more yielding mood' but he was 'rather sceptical about so rigid a mind.'[13]

There were good reasons for MacDonald's scepticism. Firstly he realised that de Valera was unlikely to give way on the annuities question. 'I think,' the Dominions Secretary noted, 'he has given a public pledge to the effect that he will never allow any of the annuities money to be paid to us, and when he has given a pledge, I am bound to say, he abides by it.'[14] Secondly, from the standpoint of an overall settlement the partition question posed even greater problems. Although de Valera had on the whole played down that issue in his public utterances while unilaterally dismantling the disagreeable aspects of the Treaty, privately he had left the British in no doubt that it was a major concern. 'Throughout all my conversations with him during the last two years,' MacDonald informed his colleagues, 'he has been at pains to emphasise in his view that no final settlement of the relations between the two countries is possible whilst partition remains.'[15] Thirdly, the Irish leader made it clear that he wanted the unconditional handing over of the Treaty ports.

Anxious that the country should be in the position of being able to remain neutral in the event of another major war, de Valera contended that Ireland should be free to decide whether or not bases should be made available to Britain. While he could not give an assurance, he said he thought that Dublin would hand over the ports. If Ireland had been free in 1914, for example, he explained that he would probably have volunteered to fight in Flanders himself.[16] He went on to indicate in subsequent conversations that he was prepared to guarantee that Ireland could never be used as a base for an attack on Britain, and that if some country attacked Ireland in an effort to obtain just such a base, he would invite the British to defend her. Thus while the British would not have a guarantee of being able to use an Irish base, they would at least have an assurance of a benevolent Irish neutrality. 'I am convinced,' MacDonald wrote after his meeting with the Irish leader on 6 October 1937, 'that he is really genuine in desiring whole-hearted friendship and co-operation between the Irish Free State and Great Britain.'[17]

During the same meeting de Valera actually contended that the settlement of Anglo-Irish differences would have a broader significance in that it would lead to better relations between the United States and Britain by, in effect, diffusing the anglophobia of Irish-Americans. He indicated, according to MacDonald, that 'real unqualified friendship with the United States would be vastly more valuable to Britain than the satisfaction of a claim of money, or the British occupation of the three Irish ports against the will of almost the whole Southern Irish population.'

Before leaving for the Anglo-Irish talks, which began in London on 17 January 1938, de Valera sought American assistance. He explained to John Cudahy, the United States Minister in Dublin, that American opinion could have a tremendous bearing on the outcome of the talks. In fact, five months earlier during their first meeting, de Valera told Cudahy, who was the first Irish-American to be appointed to the post in Dublin, that 'without the moral support of American public opinion the Irish Free State could never have become a reality.'[18] It was now obvious that the Irish leader was anxious to enlist the same kind of moral support for his continuing struggle with the British. He suggested that Joseph P. Kennedy, whose appointment as Ambassador to Britain had recently been announced in Washington, could be of great assistance.[19] It seemed propitious indeed that an Irish-American should be appointed to the London post at such a time, especially as there was another Irish-American already in Dublin.

At the outset of the London talks de Valera, who was accompanied by Lemass, MacEntee, and Ryan, was called upon to set the order of business. He responded by putting all the issues into the context of overall defence. He not only referred to partition in the sense that its continuance would prevent Irish co-operation with Britain in the event of war, but added that the occupation of the three Irish ports posed a great danger to both countries, because the issue acted as a distraction on preparations for Ireland's defence. If that distraction were eliminated, then Irish authorities could go about enthusiastically mustering the Irish people in preparation for their own defence. The Taoiseach firmly believed that this was not only in Ireland's interest but also that of Britain, on the grounds that the best guarantee they could have on their Irish flank was a friendly and contented Ireland, whose people would then have something really worth fighting for, if some country tried to use the island as a base for an attack on Britain. He even managed to fit the annuities question and the resulting economic war into the context of defence by suggesting that Britain should drop not only her claims but also her duties on Irish imports so that the Dublin government could afford the funds sorely needed to prepare Irish defences.[20]

The ensuing discussions with the British delegation — which consisted of Chamberlain, MacDonald, and two former Foreign Secretaries with whom de Valera had had contact at the League of Nations, Simon, then Chancellor of the Exchequer, and Hoare, the Home Secretary — were divided into three distinct sessions. The first consisted of discussions held from 17 to 19 January 1938. The Irish delegation then returned home and there was a break of a month, during which there was a general election in Northern Ireland that predictably resulted in a comfortable victory for the Unionist Party. The second session of the formal talks was a somewhat haphazard affair disrupted by a British political crisis caused by the resignation of the Foreign Secretary, Sir Anthony Eden. Although the Irish delegation had already returned to London when the political storm erupted, it was four days before the formal talks could resume. Nevertheless MacDonald and de Valera did have some informal discussions in the interim. Following the second phase the Irish delegation again returned to Dublin, where the cabinet was brought up to date. The third session then began on 3 March and continued until 11 March 1938. The Irish delegation returned home next day with a draft treaty, but it necessitated further alterations before an agreement was finally concluded more than a month later.

The topics under discussion in London were divided into four general areas, relating to partition, defence, finance, and trade. Partition was by far the most important, according to de Valera, who repeatedly stressed that there could be no real co-operation between Dublin and London unless partition were ended. As Northern Ireland was dependent on the British, he pointed out that 'it was their business to use their influence with the Northern Ireland Government in the direction of a united Ireland.'[21]

From the outset Chamberlain's attitude was that Britain could do nothing without Belfast's approval and that 'de Valera must therefore get it out of his head any idea that anything could be done at present.' As far as the British leader was concerned, de Valera and his colleagues would have a better chance of achieving Irish unity if they conducted their policy in such a way 'as to remove the suspicion that they were drifting away from the Empire and, by entering an agreement with ourselves to show their desire for better relations.'[22]

The British quickly revealed that they were prepared to hand over the Treaty ports, although Chamberlain did ask for an assurance that Britain could use them in the event of an emergency. But de Valera was unwilling to make that concession unless partition was first ended. Without real progress on the unity question, he explained that the ports would have to be handed over unconditionally. Chamberlain then stunned the Irish delegation by suggesting that officials should draw up a defence agreement on those terms.[23]

Unknown to de Valera, the British chiefs of staff had advised that there were really only three alternatives open to their representatives: (1) they could hand over the ports in return for a formal alliance whereby Ireland would promise to make them available in time of war; (2) they could turn them over unconditionally in the hope that Ireland would be, at least, a friendly neutral in any forthcoming war; or (3) they could retain the facilities in line with the terms of the 1921 Treaty, and ignore the possibility of eventual hostilities with the Irish.[24]

The latter was the least attractive of the alternatives, as far as the chiefs of staff were concerned, because they envisioned that without Irish consent, Britain would find herself with 'a series of Gibraltars scattered round the Irish coast.' Consequently, when de Valera rejected an alliance, unless partition were ended, the British were left with the alternative of returning the ports unconditionally.

Progress was also quickly made on the financial questions with the British agreeing to wipe out the whole debt with one bulk payment. When de Valera reiterated his determination not to pay the land annuities in any form, the British indicated that they were prepared to accept that, if he would agree to pay the rest of the money that was outstanding. At the time it was estimated that the overall amount involved in the British claims was £105 millions, of which the land annuities accounted for three-quarters. Thus the British agreed to settle for £26 millions.

There had therefore been some very significant progress when the first phase of the talks ended on 19 January 1938. Chamberlain, who had obviously anticipated that negotiating with de Valera would be difficult, was certainly optimistic. Immediately before the talks began, for instance, the Prime Minister was reported to have depicted de Valera as having a 'mentality' that 'was in some ways like Herr Hitler's. It was no use employing with them the arguments which appealed to any ordinary reasonable man.'[25] Yet after the first phase of the negotiations the British leader had become convinced that although a 'queer creature' in many ways, his Irish counterpart was sincere and was 'no enemy' of Britain. Thus Chamberlain was hopeful about

the chances for a settlement. 'I shall be greviously disappointed,' he wrote in his diary, 'if we don't get an all-
round agreement on everything except partition. That is
the difference that cannot be bridged without the assent of
Ulster.' But he was confident that if de Valera accepted his
advice about eliminating the suspicion that Ireland was
breaking away from the British Commonwealth, then there
would eventually be an end to partition.[26]

Meanwhile, however, de Valera provided the American
Minister with a very gloomy account of the negotiations.
He gave no indication that the British were prepared to
drop their land annuities claim, nor that they had offered to
conclude an agreement on defence that would provide for
the return of the ports and the abrogation of the defence
provisions in the 1921 Treaty, with no obligation on the
Irish side except to agree to unfettered consultation with
Britain on defence matters. Instead he depicted the talks as
doomed to failure unless some progress could be made on
the partition question. He referred to an article in the *Irish
Independent,* the previous day, in which Mary MacSwiney
had warned against any compromise. The Taoiseach
explained to Cudahy that 'Irish sentiment would be overwhelmingly against any co-operation with England while
Ireland is disunited by partition.'[27] Consequently, he predicted that any Irish leader who tried to compromise would
be repudiated.[28]

Cudahy was sympathetic with de Valera's aims because
he believed that Anglo-Irish rapproachement would have
favourable consequences for the United States in that it
would secure 'the approval by a great share of American
public opinion of closer American-British relations.' The
American Minister therefore suggested that President
Roosevelt should talk with the British Ambassador in
Washington. 'I believe,' he wrote to the President, 'if you
saw Sir Ronald Lindsay at the White House and told him
you were interested in the settlement of the Anglo-Irish
differences, and hoped the present negotiations might succeed, the effect would be conclusive for success.'[29]

'The British Ambassador will tell you he can do nothing,
that the question of Ulster and Irish unity must be settled

by Ulster and that London can have nothing to do with it,' Cudahy continued. 'But if Mr Chamberlain sends for Lord Craigavon the leader of the Ulster Party and appealing to him as a patriot tells him that the defence of England is at stake, the result will be surprising.' He explained that the British were in a position to put pressure on Belfast if they wished, by withdrawing British forces from the Six Counties and by suspending the financial subsidies without which, he was convinced, Stormont would collapse. The American Minister stressed, of course, that he was thinking of the question from his own country's standpoint. 'I look at the whole matter,' he assured Roosevelt, 'from an objective American angle and am sure you see the far reaching significance of Irish-English friendship and co-operation for the peace of the world.'

In addition to enlisting Cudahy's help, de Valera also sent Frank Gallagher to the United States as an emissary to secure further American support for an Anglo-Irish settlement. While in Washington, Gallagher received a sympathetic hearing from the influential Irish-American Senator, David I. Walsh of Massachusetts, the chairman of the Senate Naval Affairs Committee,[30] and also delivered a letter from the Taoiseach to President Roosevelt.

In that letter de Valera explained that partition was the only remaining obstacle preventing the ending of the centuries-long quarrel between Britain and Ireland. 'The British Government alone have the power to remove this obstacle,' he wrote. 'If they really have the will they can bring about a united Ireland in a very short time. I have pressed my views upon them, but it is obvious that they recognise only the difficulties and are not fully alive to the great results that would follow a complete reconciliation between the two peoples. Reconciliation would affect every country where the two races dwell together, knitting their national strength and presenting to the world a great block of democratic peoples interested in preservation of Peace.'[31]

'Knowing your own interest in this matter,' the Taoiseach continued, 'I am writing to ask you to consider whether you could not use your influence to get the British

Government to realise what would be gained by reconciliation and to get them to move whilst there is time. In a short while, if the present negotiations fail, relations will be worsened.' He added that Gallagher could answer any question that Roosevelt might have about the issue.

The American President's initial reaction on receiving Cudahy's request had been to do nothing. Although Roosevelt believed that a 'final solution' of Anglo-Irish difficulties would be an 'immeasurable gain from every point of view,' he did not think that his intervention would accomplish what Cudahy had in mind. 'In the long run considerations of national defence may well lead England voluntarily to take the action you now urge us to advocate,' he explained. 'She is not blind to such considerations, but I feel it would be a healthier solution, even if a slower one, if her decision were reached voluntarily, and on the basis of her own self-interest, than as a result of representations from a third power.'[32]

Having received the Taoiseach's letter, however, Roosevelt had a change of heart. He decided to intervene discreetly by asking his newly appointed Ambassdor to Britain to make informal representations to Chamberlain. 'You will realise, I know, that I cannot officially or through diplomatic channels accomplish anything or even discuss the matter,' the President wrote to de Valera on 22 February 1938. 'But I have taken the course of asking my friend, Mr Joseph P. Kennedy, who sails today for England to take up his post as Ambassador, to convey a personal message from me to the Prime Minister, and to tell the Prime Minister how happy I should be if reconciliation could be brought about.'

Next day when the talks reconvened in London, de Valera reaffirmed his stand on the need to end partition. He contended that the British were directly responsible for the mess, so the Irish people would not tolerate any government in Dublin that concluded a defence agreement with Britain, even on the innocuous terms offered. Without a commitment on the unity issue, he explained that he and his colleagues could not assume the responsibility for sponsoring any such agreement.

Chamberlain explained his own difficulties on the Ulster question in very much the same terms. He impressed de Valera with his candour in privately admitting that while he personally considered partition an anachronism, he could do nothing about it because British public opinion would not stand for putting pressure on Belfast in the matter.

When asked to suggest a way out of the impasse, de Valera replied that the British should just hand over the ports without any defence agreement, and that the two sides might settle the financial dispute and come to some trade agreement. But he rejected the idea of giving preferential treatment to imports from Northern Ireland in return for the ports. As far as the Irish people were concerned, the Taoiseach said, the ports were theirs by right, with the result that they would not tolerate making any concessions to Britain for returning what had rightfully belonged to Ireland in the first place.

Before returning home after the session de Valera and Seán MacEntee received a deputation of Nationalists from the Six Counties in their London hotel. The deputation urged the Taoiseach to take a firm stand on the partition issue. 'We would regard it as a betrayal of our interests if he ignored the problem of partition by getting trade and defence agreements only,' Cahir Healy, the Nationalist leader, explained to the press afterwards.

There could be little doubt that de Valera welcomed the appearance of being under pressure from his own people to follow a hardline, because it enforced his contention of being unable to bargain on other issues while partition lasted. During the break between the first and second phases of the negotiations, he had undoubtely helped to rouse public interest in partition by giving interviews to correspondents of the *New York Times*, International News Service, and the *Manchester Guardian*. These interviews, in which, he emphasised the partition issue, were given prominence in Irish newspapers, especially his own *Irish Press*. The resulting publicity, followed so closely by the visit of the Nationalist deputation undoubtedly helped to further de Valera's efforts to depict the issue as one on which the Dublin government was hamstrung.

Thus when the third session of the talks began on 3 March 1938, the Taoiseach again emphasised that his hands were tied by partition. He refused to make any trade concessions to Northern Ireland because of the discrimination against the nationalist minority in the area. If preference were given to the North's industries, he said that the infant industries recently established in the Twenty-six Counties would suffer. While he would be willing to face that problem if partition were ended, he would not in the existing situation. The only suggestion that he could therefore offer was the possibility of exchanging preferential treatment in the trade of certain items.

With the British depending on obtaining significant trade concessions in order to alleviate parliamentary opposition to the handing over of the ports, Chamberlain suggested that if Dublin made such concessions to Belfast, it might lead to improved relations and thereby help to break down the barriers of partition. He was obviously looking for something in return for his gesture of handing over the ports.

Here de Valera showed himself as a masterly tactician. Having earlier argued that he could make no concession for the ports because Britain was only returning what rightfully belonged to Ireland, he now went a step further and sought to improve his bargaining position by turning the tables on Chamberlain and demanding a concession from the British for Dublin's willingness to take the ports off their hands. To the utter amazement of the British leader, de Valera explained that it was not at all certain that the Irish people would welcome the handing over of the ports, because they realised that it would mean that Dublin would have to assume the financial burden of defending them.

'I am lost in admiration for Mr de Valera's skill in dialectics,' the surprised Chamberlain told his cabinet. He then added sarcastically that it might have been better 'to spare Mr de Valera the embarrassment of having the Treaty ports offered to him.'[33]

Notwithstanding his historical image as a weak and vacillating leader, Chamberlain could be a tough, hard-headed politician, and he began to dig his own heels in. On 8 March he told de Valera in no uncertain terms that there could be no question of handing over the ports or any trade or financial agreements unless Dublin were prepared to offer trade concessions to Northern Ireland.[34] He emphasised those conditions again three days later on presenting de Valera with draft terms for an agreement.

Next day, 12 March 1938, the Irish delegation returned to Dublin to consider the British proposals, which offered to abrogate unconditionally the defence articles of the 1921 Treaty, and to settle the financial dispute in return for a lump-sum payment of £10 millions by the Dublin government. The British also offered a trade agreement under which their levies on Irish imports would be abolished and, in return, Ireland would review her own tariffs on British imports and in some cases afford Britain preferential treatment. In addition, Dublin would reduce its duties on imports from the Six Counties immediately, and would eliminate those duties completely within four years. The draft terms also contained a British offer to declare that while there could be no change in Northern Ireland's status without her own consent, Britain would lend active assistance if Stormont desired closer relations with the Twenty-six Counties.

Under instructions from de Valera, John Dulanty told MacDonald that the British terms were unacceptable two days later. 'The provisions put forward late in the negotiations about our making big concessions to the North had made the proposals completely impossible for the Government of Eire,' Dulanty reportedly told the Dominions Secretary. 'It might well be that our people could have accepted the other items, even though nothing had been done on the question of partition, but so long as the minority in the Six Counties is treated as it is today, any concession to the Six Counties would be a sheer impossibility,' he added that the statement regarding partition 'was altogether inadequate.'[35]

In Dublin, meanwhile, de Valera told Cudahy that the talks 'had utterly collapsed'.[36] But it was at this point that Roosevelt's intervention began to pay off. Ambassador Kennedy told Dulanty next day that he had just delivered

the American President's message and had explained to
Chamberlain that Roosevelt was of the opinion that an
Irish settlement was a matter of importance to Anglo-
American co-operation.[37]

When the British cabinet met to discuss the situation on
13 April 1938, Chamberlain explained that Kennedy 'had
spoken strongly to him of the valuable effect on opinion in
America of an agreement with Éire.'[38] The Prime Minister
of Northern Ireland, Lord Craigavon (formerly Sir James
Craig), had already opened the door for the British to
backdown by intimating that instead of trade concessions
from Dublin, he would be satisfied if Northern Ireland
were awarded some of the arms contracts that were being
made as Britain prepared militarily for war. The cabinet
therefore decided to drop the demand that Dublin make
trade concessions to Northern Ireland. Just what impact
the American President's message actually had in the eventual decision is, of course, impossible to gauge, but it seems
that de Valera himself believed that it had a very significant
impact.

'The knowledge of the fact that you were interested
came most opportunely at a critical moment in the progress
of the negotiations,' de Valera wrote to Roosevelt after the
agreement was reached but before it was actually signed.
'Were it not for Mr Chamberlain personally the negotiations would have broken down at that time, and I am sure
that the knowledge of your interest in the success of the
negotiations had its due weight in determining his attitude.'
While both countries would look with satisfaction on the
agreement, which was signed in London three days later,
de Valera warned that it really did nothing about partition,
which was the issue that affected Irish national sentiment
most. Consequently complete reconciliation had not yet
been achieved. 'All we can hope,' the Taoiseach wrote, 'is
that the present agreement will be a step towards it.'[39]

Cudahy was jubilant over the agreement. 'I think,' he
explained to Roosevelt, 'this agreement will have more far-
reaching significance for world peace than is now recognised and certainly from an American viewpoint it is a very
desirable accomplishment. I am certain the Irish-American

element will acclaim it more enthusiastically even than here in Ireland, especially the abandonment of the ports by the British.'[40]

The settlement was 'a wonderful triumph for de Valera,' according to the American Minister, who considered the Taoiseach 'a genius as a negotiator for he refused in telling me about the terms of the agreement to become jubilant and no doubt he gave the impression in London of getting nothing.'[41] Shortly afterwards Cudahy reported that de Valera had privately told him that a great deal of the credit was due to the British leader for having 'accomplished wonders in persuading his associates to make concessions in favour of Ireland,' but he added that he could not publicly compliment Chamberlain for fear of being criticised for being 'too friendly' to Britain.[42]

The Taoiseach had met with some opposition to the agreements. One former Fianna Fáil minister vigorously urged him to reject the British terms. 'I am afraid,' Belfast-born Joe Connolly recalled, 'I argued rather vehemently that, if the partition of the country was not solved then when the other matters were being settled, the prospects of having it raised and decided in the near future were not very bright.'[43]

De Valera therefore played down the agreement on presenting it to the Dáil. He said, for instance, that the financial settlement, in which the British had written off more than ninety per cent of their claim, was not a good one. 'I have repeatedly stated my belief,' he added, 'that, if we were making agreements on the basis of justice — if sheer equity was to decide these matters — instead of paying money to Britain, whether a big or small sum, the payments should be made the other way.' He added that Dáil deputies could, if they wished, regard the Irish payment 'as ransom money'.[44]

In regard to the ports, he declared that they were being handed over unconditionally, but added that, 'as a matter of right,' they had always belonged to Ireland anyway. 'We are glad,' he said, 'that that right has been recognised and that now we are to have them.' The most positive thing he had to say about the agreements was that they had opened the way for the country to concentrate on ending partition. 'These agreements, as a whole,' he explained, 'will remove from the field of dispute between Great Britain and ourselves all the major items now, except that one. The whole Irish race can now concentrate upon that one.'

The agreements were received with such enthusiasm by the public that de Valera called a general election having lost a minor vote in the Dáil in May 1938. Although he adopted a statesmanlike stance himself during the campaign, his deputy leader, Seán T. O'Kelly, took a somewhat demagogic approach. 'I think,' he told an election rally in Dublin, for example, 'that no one will doubt that England and the British Empire is a very powerful — if not the most powerful — political force in the world today, and in the past six years look how we whipped John Bull every time. Look at the last agreement we made with her. We won all round us, we wiped her right, left and centre, and, with God's help, we shall do the same again.'[45]

Fianna Fáil secured a resounding election victory. In fact, its fifteen seat majority in the new Dáil was the largest that the party was ever able to enjoy during de Valera's lifetime.

Although the Anglo-Irish agreements of 1938 revised the disagreeable aspects of the 1921 Treaty, there still remained the question of partition to be settled, and there was also a doubt in many people's minds whether a dominion had a right to remain neutral. This was important at the time, because Europe was obviously moving closer to war every month. During the Anglo-Irish negotiation there had been some major international developments — most notable of which was Hitler's invasion and annexation of Austria. But de Valera paid little attention to such developments.[46] His attitude then and later was to avoid involvement, if possible. Publicly he reaffirmed his intention of remaining neutral in the event of war.

'We do not wish to get into a war if we can keep out of it,' he told the Dáil on 13 July 1938. Not only did he not intend being obligated to fight in defence of the Covenant of the League of Nations, but he also made it clear that Ireland's relationship with the British Commonwealth would not affect the Dublin government's freedom of action in any future dispute. 'Constitutionally,' he explained, 'I want every deputy to realise that we have no commitments, we can keep out of war, we can be neutral if we want.' The leaders of the dominions had 'very defintely stated' that they could not be committed to war, or indeed committed to any course of action in advance, without their own approval. And so it was also with Ireland. 'We are exactly in that situation,' de Valera declared. The Irish parliament would be free to act as it saw fit when any crisis occurred.

Of course, simply announcing that the country intended to remain neutral would not necessarily keep Ireland out of the war. That would depend to a great extent on whether other countries were willing to respect Irish neutrality. There was always the danger that Ireland would be attacked. He felt that such an attack could fall into one of two categories. The first would be a British assault. Although he did not rule out that possibility, he did say that he thought it unlikely.

'I think that with the progress of events and the direction in which we are are travelling, and in which the world is travelling, that it is not likely to happen,' he said. Consequently, the Taoiseach was really only afraid of the other category of attack in which a state other than Britain, such as a large unnamed continental power, would be the aggressor. If such an attack took place, he obviously intended to rely on Britain for help, because he was convinced that once the British thought their situation would be affected by another country occupying Ireland, then they would 'be interested in giving to us any aid that we might ask.' If such an assault became likely, he even suggested that Dublin might be willing to engage in consultations with the British in advance.[47]

While he said nothing that indicated publicly that he would be willing to abandon neutrality without being compelled to do so, his general tone towards Britain demonstrated the marked improvement in relations between Dublin and London since the Anglo-Irish agreements were signed a few weeks earlier. And there was evidence that this rapproachement was mutual when, in September

1938, the British promoted de Valera's successful candidacy for the Presidency of the nineteenth Assembly of the League of Nations.

The autumn of 1938 was, in de Valera's own words, 'a time of unparalleled anxiety' for the people of Europe.[48] The Assembly convened during the Sudeten crisis and sat through the talks which led to the Munich Agreement of 1938. With Hitler threatening to seize the Sudetenland of Czechoslovakia, there was an air of foreboding when de Valera delivered his presidential address to the Assembly.

In that address he emphasised the futility of war, which was so tragically demonstrated during the First World War. 'We have experienced its horrors and seen around us the havoc which it wrought,' he said. 'The twenty years of exhaustion and penury which the peoples have had to endure since its termination, and the uncertainty of the present hour, proclaim how little the sufferings and the sacrifices of its terrible years have availed in providing a solution to the fundamental problems of our human society.'

'All history tells us that, in the long run, to be just is to be truly wise,' he added. 'But we seem unable to apply the lesson. The circumstances of war are such that the settlements imposed by it are almost inevitably unjust. It was true in the past; it will, I fear, be true in the future, no matter whose is the victory.' He therefore suggested that the League should dedicate itself to securing a just settlement of immediate difficulties and make a beginning towards the convening of a peace conference 'upon the basis of justice which the peoples of the world want and which is possible before, but scarcely ever possible after, a war.'[49]

Years earlier de Valera had criticised the cynical manner in which the postwar treaties had divided up territory without proper regard for the wishes of inhabitants. He saw the current crisis as a logical consequence of the earlier mistakes. He was convinced that there was justice in Hitler's claims to the Sudetenland. In fact, during a stop-over in London while on his way to Geneva, he actually compared the Sudeten question to the Ulster problem by telling Sir Thomas Inskip that the Dublin government had its 'own

Sudetens in Northern Ireland'. He added that he sometimes thought 'of the possibility of going over the boundary
and pegging out the territory, just as Hitler was doing,
which was occupied by a population predominantly in sympathy with Éire.'[50]

The Taoiseach considered making a direct appeal to
Hitler, but this was obviated by Chamberlain's decision to
go to Berchtesgarten. On hearing the news of that decision,
de Valera was at a dinner in Geneva, where he supposedly
remarked that this was 'the best thing that England's ever
done'.[51] He sent a congratulatory message to Chamberlain,
assuring him that 'one person at least is completely satisfied
that you are doing the right thing — no matter what the
result.'[52]

In response, Chamberlain let it be known that he 'would
be very grateful for any steps' that de Valera might take to
mobilise opinion within the Assembly for a settlement.[53]
There was really no need to ask, because the Irish leader
was himself anxious for a settlement, but he wanted it to be
based on justice not simply a surrender to the naked threat
of Nazi aggression. When the Poles and Hungarians put
forward claims to Czechoslovakian territory, he supported
them by telling a member of the British delegation that it
was important to 'face up to the necessity of doing something to meet those Polish and Hungarian claims which can
be regarded as having a similar basis to German claims.
Otherwise the solution will stand out not as an attempt to
secure justice but a surrender.'[54] De Valera therefore
suggested that 'before there is a complete smash up, every
effort should be made to induce' President Roosevelt to
take an initiative such as 'calling a Conference to dispose of
the question at issue.'[55]

Next day de Valera delivered a radio address to the
United States over Radio Nations, reiterating his call for a
peace conference. Even if the Sudeten crisis were amicably
settled, he warned that there would not always be a man
like Neville Chamberlain who would swallow his pride and
go to the potential enemy in an effort to secure peace. 'The
time for something like a general European Peace Conference, or at least a conference between the greater powers,

is overdue,' he declared. 'If nations be called to make certain sacrifices at such a conference, these will be far less than the sacrifices they will have to make in the event of war. Settlements based on justice and fair play will allow nations that are at the moment consumed with anxiety to rest their nights in peace.'[56]

Although there was simplistic optimism in de Valera's sentiments, it was mixed with realistic assessment. He knew that the potential aggressor might not be satisfied with everything to which it was justly entitled. It might still wage war anyway, but then it would be clearly exposed as a bully. He felt that fighting such a war should not be feared as much as fighting a war in which people believed that the aggressor did have a legitimate grievance. 'If by conceding the claims of justice or by reasonable compromise in a spirit of fair play we take steps to avoid the latter kind of war,' de Valera told his American audience, 'we can face the possibility of the other kind with relative equanimity. Despite certain preaching mankind *has* advanced, and the public conscience, in a clear case of aggression, will count, and may well be in a European war a decisive factor.' It was not that he thought that peace-loving people should always surrender to those who would not be deterred by the horrors of war, but that they should 'concede unhesitatingly the demands of justice' and then adopt a policy of wait and see. 'To allow fears for the future to intervene and make us halt in rendering justice in the present, is not to be wise but to be foolish.'

Whether this speech had any impact may be open to question, because even though Roosevelt did send a message to Hitler next day encouraging him to ensure 'a peaceful, fair and constructive settlement', the White House had been considering that message for some days. Nevertheless de Valera's effort was part of his broader attempt to mobilise opinion. Next day, 27 September 1938, he sent an open telegram to Chamberlain urging him to do his utmost to preserve peace. 'Let nothing daunt you or defeat you in your effort to secure peace,' he urged as Assembly President. 'The tens of millions of innocent people on both sides who have no cause against each other, but who are in danger of being hurled against each other, with no alter-native to mutual slaughter are praying that your efforts may find a way of saving them from this terrible doom.'[57]

Early on the morning of 30 September 1938 the ill-fated Munich Agreement was concluded. It was therefore to a greatly relieved Assembly that de Valera delivered the closing address later that day. Having deliberately avoided giving public credit for the Anglo-Irish agreements earlier in the year, he was now effusive in his praise of Chamber-lain, whom he described as a 'knight of peace' who had 'attained the highest peak of human greatnesss, and a glory greater than that of all the conquerors.' Although the League had played no role in the actual settlement, de Valera used the occasion for yet another appeal for the organisation's reform, so that 'in spite of present problems and difficulties, the confidence which, twenty years ago, was reposed in the League may be justified and fulfilled.' He added, however, that peace depended less 'on formal instruments than on the spirit which gives these instru-ments life. The question of national minorities has been very much before our minds in recent weeks. We have seen the danger we run by leaving these problems unsolved.' Although he admitted that there were other problems that were equally dangerous, there could be no doubt that it was the minorities problem that interested him most, because he obviously saw a golden chance to bring about Irish unity.[58]

Now that all other Anglo-Irish problems were out of the way it was possible to concentrate on partition, and the prospects of success were enhanced by the presence of a strong Conservative government in London. 'Anybody who has studied Irish history,' de Valera told the Dáil some months earlier, 'must have learned this fact, that, if ever there was to be a settlement between Ireland and Britain, that settlement would have to come in a time, not when you had a Liberal Government, but when you had a Conser-vative Government in office; because the Conservative Government, once it convinced its own people that the agreement should be come to, was not likely to be opposed by either Liberal or Labour, who themselves would have advocated such a course long before but would have been unable to carry it out.'[59] Earlier in the year Chamberlain admitted that he would like to see partition ended, but felt unable to do anything about it because of British public opinion. Since then, however, his popularity had soared as a result of the Munich Agreement, which in itself provided an apt precedent — at least as far as the Taoiseach was concerned — for ending partition.

On his way home, de Valera stopped in London and urged Chamberlain to act on the partition question, but the Prime Minister declined. Believing that this was on account of the lack of popular support, de Valera therefore set out to win the necessary public approval. On 13 October 1938 he gave a widely publicised interview to Hessel Tiltmann of the London *Evening Standard* in which he held out the possibility of concluding an alliance with Britain in return for the ending of partition.[60] Of course, he had made such an offer during the talks earlier in the year, but the significant thing was this time he talked about it publicly. He explained that it was 'possible to visualise a critical situation arising in the future in which a united Ireland would be willing to co-operate with Britain to resist a common attack.' But if partition still existed at the outbreak of another war, he warned that co-operation would be impossible because of public opinion in Ireland. If the British would only convert their friends in Northern Ireland to the idea of Irish unity on fair terms, he said, the Irish people would feel that they had something worth fighting for. But he went on to state 'no Irish leader will ever be able to get the Irish people to co-operate with Great Britain while partition remains. I wouldn't attempt it myself, for I know I should fail.'

Explaining that he wanted to see Irish unity brought about early enough so that it would be securely established before the outbreak of another major war, the Taoiseach reiterated his willingness to compromise with the Northern majority. 'Keep your local Parliament with its legal powers if you wish,' he would say to them. 'The Government of Éire asks for only two things of you. There must be adequate safeguards that the ordinary rights of the nationalist minority in your area shall not be denied them, as at present, and that the powers at present reserved to the English Parliament shall be tranferred to the all-Ireland Parliament.'

Time Magazine described the interview as a blatant attempt at blackmailing the London government by exploiting the Munich agreement. 'Obviously,' according to the magazine, 'de Valera was thinking in Czechoslovak terms' and had not made 'the slightest attempt to spare British feelings.'[61]

At the Fianna Fáil Árd Fheis a few weeks later the Taoiseach announced that he was asking AARIR — the American organisation that he had helped to found in 1920 — and the two ethnic newspapers that had consistently supported him in the United States, the New York *Irish World* and San Francisco *Leader* to help in 'making known to the American public the nature of partition and the wrong done by it to the Irish nation.' The American Minister in Dublin had no doubt that de Valera was embarking on an overall plan to marshall Irish-Americans as a force to exert pressure for Irish unity.[62]

The Taoiseach told Cudahy that the Munich settlement was an indication that orderly international negotiations were — if not dead — at least in moribund abeyance, with the result that he was anxious that Ireland should put her own house in order. He was, in effect, staking a claim for the nationalist areas of the Six Counties, just like Hitler had done with the Sudetenland. De Valera explained, for example, that the course of the Bann River could be used to draw a line to the south and west of which the majority favoured Irish unity. He therefore proposed that a plebescite should 'be conducted by voting units in rural and urban districts which alone would reveal the sentiments of Northern Ireland as a whole.'[63]

Speaking in the Senate on 7 February 1939 he admitted that he would be prepared to use force to secure Irish unity, if he thought it would be successful. 'I am not a pacifist by any means,' the Taoiseach said. 'I would, if I could see a way of doing it effectively, rescue the people of Tyrone and Fermanagh, south Down, south Armagh, and Derry City from the coercion which they are suffering at the present time, because I believe that, if there is to be no coercion that ought to apply all round.' He added that there was 'not the slightest doubt about it that if there were not British military forces in those areas, those people would move to come in with us, and we would certainly take them.'[64]

During the speech de Valera explained that he had not asked the British to coerce Northern Ireland, because he realised that members of the British government wished to see partition ended, but felt unable to act because the majority in Northern Ireland obviously wanted partition with the result that British public opinion would not tolerate efforts to compel the North to sever ties with Britain. His policy therefore was simply 'to instruct the British people'. He was not asking them 'to do anything in the way of coercing those in the North-East who do not want to come in with us but to cease actively encouraging that section to keep out.' Consequently he said that he had no apologies for using propaganda, because if force were to be ruled out, then it was necessary to use propaganda 'to appeal to common sense and to good will'.

'We have tried to inform our people,' the Taoiseach added, 'not merely here, but our own people throughout the world wherever they might be, wherever they might have a voice, and wherever they could bring their influence to bear.' The real bar to unity was the favours that the British were bestowing on Northern Ireland which, he said, had the effect of preventing the working of 'the ordinary natural laws' that would bring the two Irish communities together. 'What is the use in our holding out attractions to them if, when we offer something, twice as much is offered by the people who are competing.'

De Valera certainly had a good case, especially in calling for the transfer of the nationalist areas. There was no valid, moral justification for compelling those areas to remain within Northern Ireland. Even Frank MacDermot, who had a reputation for being somewhat of an anglophile, observed that the boundary obviously ought to be revised. He therefore asked if the Taoiseach had ever requested the British to transfer the contiguous nationalist areas.

'I have not,' de Valera replied, 'because I think the time has come when we ought to do the thing properly. That would only be a half-measure.'[65] In other words he was looking for the whole of the Six Counties or nothing and was apparently making an issue of the possible transfer of nationalist areas only for propaganda purposes.

He had already admitted that the majority in Northern Ireland wanted partition, so he was opposed to using coercion to bring about unity under the circumstances. Yet over the years he did very little to try to win over the Northern majority. In fact, Seán Ó Faoláin contended in 1939 that the Dublin government had been effectively promoting partition 'by refusing to demonstrate a practical spirit of tolerance and broad-mindedness.'[66]

Ever since the foundation of the state there had been discrimination against Protestant values in such matters as divorce, birth control, and censorship. De Valera himself had become involved in a notorious instance of job discrimination in 1931 when, as Leader of the Opposition, he supported people in County Mayo who were demanding the removal of a Protestant woman as librarian. Since the librarian could be expected to recommend books to people, he thought that the post was of an educational nature. And observing that Roman Catholics had 'jealously looked after' the guardianship of education over the years, he contended that the people of Mayo, who were overwhelmingly Roman Catholic, were 'justified in insisting upon a Catholic librarian'. In addition, he also stated that such communities were entitled to insist upon the appointment of Roman Catholic doctors 'because everybody knows that at the moment of death Catholics are particularly anxious that their people be attended by Catholic doctors. I say that if I had a vote on a local body, and if there were two qualified people who had to deal with a Catholic community, and if one was a Catholic and the other a Protestant, I would unhesitatingly vote for the Catholic.'[67] If that kind of reasoning were carried to its logical conclusion it would have meant that Protestants would be debarred from a great many posts in the state.

Having come to power de Valera and his colleagues

often made the mistake of implying that 'the only true Irishmen were Catholics', but in fairness to him, he 'did not act on the doctrines which he had propounded in the Mayo library debate.'[68] In fact, he was instrumental in having the founder of the Gaelic League, Douglas Hyde, who happened to be a Protestant, selected as the first President under the 1937 constitution.

Although Fianna Fáil had not instituted the discrimination against Protestant values, de Valera's government did intensify that discrimination by extending a ban on the advertising of contraceptives, their sale and importation. In addition, divorce — hitherto illegal — was made unconstitutional in the constitution of 1937 which closely reflected Roman Catholic social teaching. Censorship reached virtual draconian proportions with many Irish writers of international distinction being banned, sometimes on ludicrous grounds. There was also institutionalised discrimination within the civil service and education system in favour of those able to use the Irish language — for which Northern unionists had little affection.

De Valera actually declared publicly that he would prefer the restoration of Irish as the everyday language of the people to the ending of partition. 'If I were told tomorrow, "You can have a united Ireland if you give up the idea of restoring the national language to be the spoken language of the majority of the people,"' he said, 'I would, for myself, say no.'[69] On another occasion he explained that if he 'had to make a choice between political freedom with the language, and the language without political freedom,' he would choose the latter. Faced with that kind of reasoning, Northern unionists could hardly be blamed for thinking that de Valera might take away their freedom within a united Ireland, if they refused to use the language. Furthermore the economic nationalism that he espoused could have little appeal for Northerners whose more industrialised economy was dependent on export markets, which could not be filled by the Twenty-six Counties.

'No Northerner,' Ó Faoláin wrote, 'can possibly like such features of Southern life, as at present constituted, as its pervasive clerical control; its censorship; its Gaelic revival; its isolationist economic policy.' He added that de Valera understood the effects of at least some of those things but had shown 'no readiness to relax any of them'.[70] In fact, the Taoiseach indicated that there was no room for further compromise on the 1937 constitution,[71] which he said was designed, as far as possible, to reconcile the conflicting aspirations between the two parts of the island.[72] Consequently he was showing little inclination to adopt policies that would at least alleviate the legitimate fears of the Northern majority and thereby make the process of reconciliation that little bit easier.

Having thus ruled out both conciliatory gestures and the use of force, how did de Valera propose to solve the problem?

When referring to the question of minorities in general back in 1934 he had explained that he thought that the best solution would be to transfer the minority to its ancestral home, if possible.[73] When applied to the Irish situation, he was not thinking of transferring the nationalists from the Six Counties, but unionists in the area to Britain. He subsequently suggested, for example, that if the Northern majority continued to refuse the offer of local autonomy in return for the transfer of powers vested in Westminster to a central Irish parliament, then there should be a solution on the lines of a provision in the Treaty of Lausanne (1923), in accordance with which Greece and Turkey exchanged certain populations. The Taoiseach believed that if no other solution could be found, then the problem could be solved by transferring Scottish-Irish Protestants from Northern Ireland to Britain and replacing them with a similar number of Roman Catholics of Irish extraction from Britain.[74]

Hence his propaganda campaign was to get 'the Irish people all over the world using whatever influence they have to try to bring partition to an end.'[75] In March he went to the Vatican for the coronation of Pope Pius XII and used the occasion to deliver a St Patrick's Day address over radio from Rome to people at home and 'especially', according to his secretary, to people of Irish birth or descent in the United States. Describing partition as 'an open wound', de Valera appealed 'to all who may hear me, and especially the millions of our race scattered throughout the world — to all who glory in the name of Ireland — to join us in a great united movement to bring it to an end.'[76]

He had already made plans to visit the United States in early May, ostensibly in order to open the Irish pavillion at the World's Fair in New York, but he told Cudahy that he planned to follow that with a six week coast-to-coast tour. With the international situation deteriorating at an alarming rate following Hitler's invasion of the rump of Czechoslovakia in March 1939, de Valera became convinced that there would be another major war in the following autumn,[77] which seemed to strengthen his chances for unity, because the British were so anxious for Anglo-American co-operation that there was a possibility of persuading them to abandon Northern Ireland in the hope of at least neutralising the traditional anglophobia of Irish-Americans, if the latter were seen to possess enough political influence to prevent Anglo-American co-operation. It was obvious that de Valera was planning a massive propaganda effort, comparable to that of 1919 when he travelled across the United States speaking against the Versailles Treaty.

Cudahy warned, however, that there was a danger of an American backlash. Although the American people wished to avoid involvement in the impending European war, he explained that they were not neutral. They were strongly sympathetic towards the democracies and would therefore resent any actions that could be interpreted as anti-British.

'I told Mr de Valera,' the American Minister reported, 'that I was certain only an insignificant, die-hard, recalcitrant Irish element would support him if he dwelt upon the partition issue during his visit to the United States. I said I was sure the great bulk of the American people would deplore the introduction of this note which they would regard as a most discordant one during this time of gravest tension in Europe. I told him that I wanted to impress upon him just as earnestly and at the same time just as kindly as I could that I spoke in the interest of Ireland when I said that if he persisted in emphasising partition this would re-act to the detriment of his own country.'[78]

Although the Taoiseach promised that whatever he would have to say 'would be said with tact and discrimination,' Cudahy remained sceptical. 'I wish,' he wrote to Roosevelt, 'you would hammer home to him the necessity of treading very lightly on any controversial issue directed against England.'[79]

Whether or not de Valera would have accepted such advice from Roosevelt must remain a matter for conjecture but, in view of his subsequent admission that enlisting American help for his efforts to end partition would have been the 'chief aim' of his tour,[80] there can be little doubt that Cudahy's advice had made little impact. But then the Taoiseach was very worried at the time.

The IRA had already declared a war of its own on Britain in January and had been engaging in a bombing campaign in English cities, so it was obvious that the organisation would align with Germany in trying to exploit Britain's difficulties in the coming war. Although de Valera believed that the Irish people would initially favour Britain at the start of the war, he warned that there was a grave danger of a repetition of the situation that had occurred during the First World War. Once the British tried to enforce conscription in Northern Ireland, he predicted that popular sentiment would turn to hostility and he and his colleagues would be confronted with a similar situation to that which confronted the Redmondites in 1918.[81] It was therefore little wonder that he was alarmed on hearing that the British were considering introducing conscription on the eve of his planned departure for the United States.

The tour was postponed and Seán T. O'Kelly was sent to New York instead. But the political crisis was quickly resolved with the exclusion of Northern Ireland from the conscription act passed at Westminster, so the American visit was rescheduled for September 1939, but it too had to be cancelled with the outbreak of war in Europe.

From de Valera's standpoint the postponement and subsequent cancellation were most inopportune. He was at the height of his international prestige and would have had a most impressive platform from which to appeal to Americans, especially Irish-Americans. As the New York-born son of American emigrants, he would have been returning not only as Taoiseach of Ireland but also as President of the League of Nations. Yet in the following months he would show that he was even more determined to keep Ireland out of the war than to end partition.

On the virtual eve of the outbreak of hostilities, he told James A. Farley, the American Postmaster General, of his determination to avoid involvement in the conflict. 'It will be a long war,' de Valera said, 'but in the final analysis, the Allied powers should win. From our point of view it will be best to stay out of the war. By doing so we will be able to keep intact and at the same time be friendly to England. We are desirous of being helpful, in this or any other crisis in so far as we are able, short of actual participation in the war. That would be ruinous for us and injurious to England.'[82] In the light of subsequent developments it would be difficult to fault the Taoiseach's judgment.

CHAPTER FOUR

Non-Belligerency

The Proof of Independence

The decision to remain neutral provided the most effective demonstration to date that Ireland, in spite of her remaining ties with the British Commonwealth, was free to determine her own foreign policy. But it was the resolute manner in which de Valera pursued that policy which provided the concrete proof of how completely independent the country had become as a political entity. For more than five years he pursued a policy that was unmistakably his own, although he was bribed, pressured, threatened, and intimidated by the various belligerents.

It would be wrong to suggest, however, that the main reason for staying out of the war was simply to demonstrate Irish freedom. The Taoiseach could easily have done that by following the example of the Canadian Prime Minister, W. L. Mackenzie King, who adopted what amounted to a token neutrality by waiting for more than a week after Britain formally declared war on Germany before asking the Canadian Parliament to follow suit.

As far as de Valera was concerned the decision to remain neutral was necessitated by a number of significant factors. Probably the most important consideration was his long held belief — expressed as early as the First World War — that it was madness for a small nation voluntarily to become involved in a conflict between major powers, because such a country would not be strong enough really to influence the outcome, and then it would be ignored at the conference table after the war. There were also other compelling reasons for remaining neutral. For one thing, the country was virtually defenceless, as it had only a tiny, poorly equipped army and practically no naval or air defences. The state of the country's defences was probably more the result of the original decision to remain neutral, than a cause of it, as although de Valera had clearly foreseen the coming of war, he had done little to prepare for it militarily. Once the war began, of course, the lack of adequate defences posed a strong argument militating against a change of policy.

Had the Irish government sought to join the British war effort, there would undoubtedly have been civil strife with the IRA, which had already been waging a bombing campaign of its own in English cities. Shortly after the war began in Europe, the IRA actually called on the Irish people to use England's difficulty as Ireland's opportunity to drive out the British and destroy the Orange ascendancy in Northern Ireland. The organisation actually tried to forge an alliance with the Nazis, but there was little Irish support for such treasonable activities.[1]

Even the German Minister in Dublin found that the vast majority of the Irish people sympathised with Britain in the struggle against Nazi Germany, but they nevertheless wanted to remain neutral.[2] They were obviously sick of internal strife and did not want to court more trouble.

De Valera could therefore have simply cited attachment to democratic principles as his government's justification for remaining neutral, but he did not adopt that approach. Instead, he emphasised in the Dáil on 2 September 1939 that the undoubted desire of the overwhelming majority of the Irish people to avoid involvement in the conflict was not the reason for his government's policy. 'It is not as representing the sentiments or feelings of our people that the Government stands before you with this policy,' he said. 'It stands before you as the guardian of the interests of our people, and it is to guard these interests as best we can that we are proposing to follow the policy.'

From the outset the Taoiseach was anxious to assure the British that Ireland's neutrality would be benevolently disposed towards them, but he was confronted with some real communications difficulties, as Britain had no representative in Ireland. This was primarily his own fault, because he had blocked the British when they wanted to appoint a High Commissioner in 1936.[3] It really did not matter before the war because he was frequently able to meet British leaders during visits to London or while in Geneva. But with the outbreak of the war it would not be possible for him to visit London without giving rise to speculation about possible collusion between the British and Irish governments, which could in turn provoke a German attack on Ireland. The Irish cabinet therefore decided on 6 September 1939 to invite the British to appoint a representative to Ireland.

Sir John Maffey, who had recently retired after a distinguished career in the colonial and diplomatic service, was therefore sent to Dublin, where he had a number of meetings with the Taoiseach which eventually culminated in his appointment as 'British Representative to Ireland'. The use of the title, Representative, was significant as a symbolic recognition of the fact that Ireland's connection with the British Commonwealth differed from that of the other dominions, seeing that representatives of Commonwealth countries serving in the dominions were accorded the title of High Commissioner. Nevertheless a somewhat analogous connection between Ireland and the Commonwealth was still maintained in that John Dulanty retained the title of High Commissioner in Britain. Moreover, having first tried to get the Canadians to adopt the title, 'Representative', de Valera agreed to the term 'High Commissioner' when they appointed their first representative to Ireland in December 1939. Thus the whole question of Ireland's actual connection with the Commonwealth, notwithstanding the country's neutrality, was to remain confused throughout the war and for sometime afterwards.

Meanwhile during his early meetings with Maffey, the Taoiseach went out of his way to stress the benevolence of Irish neutrality. He made it clear that he personally sympathised with the efforts of the British leader to avoid war. Chamberlain had, he said, 'done everything a man could do to prevent this tragedy.'[4] By going to such ends, Britain had allowed the moral issues at stake in the conflict to be clearly defined. 'England has a moral position today,' de Valera said. 'Hitler might have his early successes, but the moral position would tell.'[5]

Although the Taoiseach sympathised with the British, there were definite limits to the extent to which he was prepared to openly demonstrate it. For example, he rejected Maffey's proposal for Anglo-Irish naval co-operation in patrolling the Irish coast, but he did come up with a plan to help Britain while at the same time preserving the appearance of strict neutrality. Once Irish coast watchers located any German submarine, de Valera said, they would radio the information of its whereabouts. 'Not to you especially,' he explained. 'Your Admiralty must pick it up. We shall wireless it to the world. I will tell the German Minister of our intention to do this.'[6]

In other words the Irish defence forces would ostensibly be reporting to their headquarters on the activities of belligerents off the Irish coast, and each of the belligerents would be free to listen in to the reports. Not that this would be of much help to the Germans, who would be too far from Ireland to use the information, but the British, on the other hand, would be near enough to act.

In subsequent weeks Dublin further demonstrated the benevolence of its neutrality by allowing some British boats to be stationed in Irish waters for air-sea rescue purposes, and over seventy British vessels were repaired in Dublin with steel plates and fittings supplied by Britain. In addition, Irish authorities turned over seven modern oil tankers to British registry and complied with a British request that Ireland would not charter neutral ships except through Britain. In this way Anglo-Irish competition for neutral shipping could be eliminated in order to keep chartering rates down. Of course the latter agreement was advantageous to both countries, as was the Irish government's initial policy towards emigration.[7]

In the early years of the war no efforts were made to prevent Irish people from going to Britain to work in factories or to volunteer for British forces. The Dominions Secretary estimated in January 1942 that there were between 100,000 and 150,000 troops from the Twenty-six Counties in the British Army, while there was probably as many again working in British factories. The de Valera government, which was confronted with chronic unemployment at home, actually encouraged this emigration by ordering that the British Ministry of Labour's *National Clearing House Gazette* should be displayed at employment exchanges throughout Ireland. Later, restrictions were placed on emigration, especially from the agricultural sector, but by then Dublin had shown further benevolence towards Britain by agreeing to secret Anglo-Irish co-operation on military and intelligence matters.

The co-operation that the British wanted most, however, was not forthcoming, because de Valera was unwilling to allow Britain to use the ports which had been handed over the previous year. Winston Churchill, who became First Lord of the Admiralty immediately after the outbreak of hostilities, was particularly annoyed at this. Having vociferously denounced the handing over in 1938, he was not prepared simply to accept the situation. If the German U-boat campaign in the Atlantic became particularly menacing, then he was convinced that Britain 'should coerce' the Irish for use of the harbours. In the interim he ordered that 'The Admiralty should never cease to formulate through every channel its complaints' about the denial of the facilities, 'and I will from time to time bring our grievances before the cabinet. On no account must we appear to acquiesce in, still less be contented with, the odious treatment we are receiving.'[8]

In October 1939 Churchill actually suggested to the cabinet that Britain should seize Irish bases, but Anthony Eden, then Dominions Secretary cautioned moderation. He warned his colleagues that de Valera would react by appealing to world opinion on moral grounds and would thereby alienate not only the Irish people from Britain, but also many in the dominions and the United States. Churchill obviously appreciated the logic of Eden's argument because he suggested that Britain should not move against Ireland until the United States Congress could act on President Roosevelt's request for changes in American neutrality laws. After much discussion the Chamberlain cabinet decided to do nothing about Churchill's proposed seizure of Irish bases, until the matter became a question of life or death for Britain.

Though the German Minister in Dublin feared that Britain would seize Irish ports, he found that the Irish did not seem very anxious during the early months of the war. They were obviously confident that Britain would be reluctant to violate Irish neutrality for fear of undermining her moral position and thus damaging her popular support in the United States. Joseph Walshe, the Secretary of the Department for External Affairs, made it clear to the German Minister that the Irish government would indeed appeal for American help if Britain invaded.

During the period of the 'phoney war' that followed the fall of Poland, the Taoiseach concentrated on domestic affairs, especially the threat posed by the IRA's efforts to exploit Britain's difficulties. He refused to preside over, or even to take part in, the opening of a special session of the Assembly of the League of Nations which met in December 1939 to consider the Soviet Union's invasion of Finland. Cudahy tried to persuade him to go to Geneva on the grounds that there was a chance of securing 'colossal publicity' on 'a platform which would command world attention'. He would there be able 'to strike out and say that morality among nations did count and was still a power to be reckoned with.'[9]

But de Valera rejected the idea. If he talked about Finland, he said that he would also have to talk about Poland and the other areas invaded by the Nazis, which might then involve Ireland in the war with Germany. 'There is no use in an oration at this time,' he emphasised. There had already been too much talk and 'what was required if the civilisation of Europe was to be saved was action.'

According to the American Minister, de Valera spoke 'very bitterly and cynically of the League, describing it as "debris". The only country which could possibly speak with any effectiveness, he said, was the United States, and that would do no good' unless the Americans were prepared to 'follow their words with actions'. The Taoiseach added 'with mordant bitterness' that the only language of persuasion at the time was 'Tanks, Bombs, and Machine Guns'. Concluding as his 'voice shook with agitation', he said that he felt 'like a man behind a glass wall witnessing the destruction of everything he held dear, but absolutely paralysed and impotent to take any action to avert universal destruction.'[10]

This basic attitude of impotence towards the international crisis continued until the German invasion of the Low Countries in May 1940. Then de Valera turned to the United States and asked for an American declaration of support for Irish neutrality. He candidly admitted that what he would really like was an American commitment to defend Ireland, but realising that it was out of the question, he hoped that Roosevelt might be prepared simply to declare that the United States was deeply interested in the preservation of the status quo in regard to Ireland, in view of her strategic location commanding the North Atlantic trade route both by sea and air.[11]

The Americans rejected the request on 22 May 1940 on the grounds that it might be construed as a departure from the country's announced policy of avoiding involvement in the European conflict. That same day was a particularly eventful one for the Irish authorities as the real gravity of the country's precarious position was brought home. Not only did the United States make it clear that she was unwilling to become involved on Ireland's behalf, but Irish authorities came across evidence that a member of the IRA in Dublin had been harbouring a German spy, who had collected information on the disposition of Irish defence forces. Among the spy's papers were some crude plans for a German invasion of Northern Ireland to be conducted with help from the IRA in the Twenty-six Counties.

De Valera's reaction was swift. He sent Joseph Walshe to London in order to reassure the British that the Dublin government would resist any German invasion and would invite British help in repelling the invader. Walshe was also instructed to propose the holding of secret staff talks between British and Irish military personnel to plan for a co-ordinated resistance to a German incursion.

At home the Taoiseach sought to bolster the country's defences in several ways. An earnest recruiting drive was launched to strengthen the defence forces, and frantic efforts were made to purchase weapons from Britain and the United States. Potential German collaborators were rounded up as hundreds of suspected members of the IRA were interned without trial in a concentration camp at the Curragh. Moreover a Defence Conference consisting of representatives of the three major parties in the Dáil was established ostensibly to advise the government on defence matters but, more importantly, as a show of national solidarity behind the government's efforts to stay out of the war.

On 1 June 1940 de Valera went on national radio to warn the Irish people that they should 'recognise that when great powers are locked in mortal combat the rights of small nations are as naught to them. The only thing that counts,' he said, 'is how one may secure an advantage over the other, and, if the violation of our territory promises such an advantage, then our territory will be violated, our country will be made a cockpit, our homes will be levelled, and our people slaughtered.' He added that 'internal division' posed the greatest danger, 'for assuredly in this hour if we do not in our several sections hang together we shall indeed hang separately.'

On the diplomatic front Dublin sought assurances from the belligerents that they would respect Ireland's neutrality. After the German Minister, Edouard Hempel, had told Walshe that it would be impossible for Berlin to give such a guarantee under existing circumstances, de Valera warned Hempel next day that Ireland was determined to resist any attack. He made it clear that if Germany invaded, then Dublin would invite British help, and if Britain attacked first, then he would call on the Germans for assistance.

In effect de Valera was threatening the Germans with the British. He went so far as to tell the Italian Minister that the discovery of the German spy had so shattered his confidence in the willingness of the Axis powers to respect Irish neutrality that he now needed some guarantee in order to withstand the pressure that the British were exerting on him to co-operate with them. Since Italy never posed any real danger to Ireland, the Taoiseach was undoubtedly using the Italian Minister to pass on to his German colleague what amounted to a warning that the Irish government might succumb to British pressure unless Germany were prepared to promise not to attack Ireland.

The ploy obviously worked because on 1 July 1940 Hempel advised his government to promise to respect Irish neutrality. The German Foreign Minster responded ten days later with instructions for Hempel to stress in all his conversations that, 'as long as Ireland conducts herself in a neutral fashion it can be counted on with absolute certainty that Germany will respect her neutrality unconditionally.'

Efforts to obtain a similar British guarantee, however, were unsuccessful. The British cabinet actually discussed the possibility of seizing Irish bases on 16 June 1940. At the time it had before it a message from the South African Prime Minister Jan Christian Smuts, who advocated that 'the Irish Atlantic ports should be seized at once, even in the face of Irish opposition.' But Churchill was opposed to the suggestion on the grounds that such a move might have undesirable repercussions in the United Sates. 'Although as a last resort we should not hesitate to secure the ports by force,' he told his colleagues, 'it would be unwise at this moment to take any action that might compromise our position with the United States of America, in view of the present delicate developments.'[12]

Instead of acting as Smuts had suggested, the British decided to try to negotiate with Dublin for the use of the ports. Neville Chamberlain, who had resigned as Prime Minister the previous month, was selected to direct the talks. When de Valera declined to meet him in London, Malcolm MacDonald, then Minister of Health in the Churchill government, was sent to Dublin as an emissary. The British hoped that the combination of Chamberlain and MacDonald would be able to win over the Irish leader in view of their roles in the events leading to the 1938 agreements.

When MacDonald put forward a plan whereby arrangements would be made to end partition if Dublin joined the British war effort, the proposal — which will be discussed at great length in the next chapter — was rejected. De Valera explained that the only solution to the problem would be for Northern Ireland to withdraw from the war, declare neutrality, and then unite with the rest of the island. In return, the new all-Ireland parliament could consider declaring war on the Axis powers. While he did not rule out the possibility that such a declaration would be adopted, he warned that it would probably be defeated, even if he supported it himself.

Probably at no stage of the war did Ireland seem in more danger than in the first week of July 1940, when de Valera formally rejected the British overtures. On the one hand the Germans were deliberately creating the impression that they were about to invade, and on the other hand, there was grave concern lest the British should launch an attack of their own simply to forestall the suspected German invasion.

Numerous factors combined to create the Irish concern. Only a few days earlier, for example, Hitler had ordered that 'all available information media' should indicate that a German invasion of Ireland was imminent.[13] The British, in turn, responded by stepping up their preparations to use troops stationed in Northern Ireland to repel any German attack on the island. These preparations caused a near state of panic in Dublin when Irish authorities arrested a British army officer who had been gathering information to be used by British troops in the Twenty-six Counties.

About the same time Irish intelligence got hold of a British plan for the invasion of Ireland. Fears that the British would invade when their unity proposal was formally rejected on 4 July were exacerbated when Churchill announced to the House of Commons that Britain had attacked the French fleet at Oran that morning in order to prevent it from falling into German hands. In the same speech he added that 'every preparation in our power' was being made 'to repel the assaults of the enemy whether they be directed upon Great Britain or upon Ireland — which all Irishmen without distinction of creed or party, should realise is in imminent danger.' Since he had been willing to order an attack on the French — until so recently Britain's principal ally — in order to prevent French ships from falling into German hands, there could be little doubt that he would be prepared to attack Ireland to prevent the

Germans getting a foothold there.

The Irish army was therefore put on alert, and de Valera issued a statement emphasising that the government was 'resolved to maintain and defend the country's neutrality in all circumstances.'[14] Next day he stressed the same theme in an interview with Harold Denny of the *New York Times*. 'We do not have the slightest intention of abandoning our neutrality,' he said. 'We intend to resist any attack, from any quarter whatever.' He added that 'strict neutrality is our best safeguard. If we let one country in, that inevitably would provoke the other to attack. Our only hope is to let none in.'[15]

During the interview the Taoiseach left no doubt that he believed that most Irish people were opposed to the Nazis. 'Probably few are actually pro-Germans,' he explained, 'for many Irishmen realise that the Irish with their passion for individualism are the last people in the world who could endure fascist rule. But in some sections of the population one finds greater bitterness against Britain than is realised outside.' In short, de Valera was contending that residual anglophobic bitterness which was being perpetrated by partition and which he described as the only question between Britain and Ireland which had not been amicably settled, had left the Dublin government with no choice but to remain neutral.

The interview with the American correspondent was basically designed to deter a British invasion of Ireland by reminding the American people that the Irish, like themselves, were determined to stay out of the war. Under the circumstances, therefore, a British attack would make Churchill look little better than Hitler and would thereby give impetus to isolationist sentiment in the United States which, in turn, could undermine vital American aid to Britain.

De Valera's tactics worked. Secretary of State Hull warned the British Ambassador in Washington that a British attack on Ireland could have disastrous consequences for Anglo-American relations and prove very embarrassing for Roosevelt's pro-British policies, especially in an election year in which the President was running for an unprecedented third term. In reply, the Ambassador gave an assurance that Britain would undertake no such venture unless the Germans attacked first.

Yet at no time during the war were the British willing to assure de Valera that they would respect Irish neutrality. The Taoiseach complained to Maffey on 17 July 1940 that Dublin had initially been primarily concerned about the danger of a German invasion, but had become even more worried about a British assault in recent weeks. The activities of the British spy were the cause for particular concern, he explained. The Irish had already shown their defences to the British and had revealed their plans for coping with a German attack, therefore Irish officers could not understand why the spy had been sent, unless it was to prepare for a British assault. In addition there was uneasiness over the British plan for an invasion of Ireland.

Maffey responded that the invasion document was only a contingency plan, and that the spy had simply been seeking information for use in case British troops were invited into the Twenty-six Counties. The British Representative apologised for the whole affair and said that it did not have the blessing of the War Office in London. Promising that it would not happen again, he asked for the release of the officer concerned.

Satisfied with the explanation, de Valera agreed to free the man. The Taoiseach undoubtedly hoped that his conciliatory gesture might be reciprocated because he then proceeded to make a moving appeal for weapons. 'Give us help with arms and we will fight the Germans as only Irishmen in their own country can fight,' he said. 'There is no doubt on which side my sympathies lie. Nowadays some people joke about my becoming pro-British. The cause I am urging on you is in the best interest of my country and this is what matters most to me.'

Maffey's report of the meeting made a good impression on the Dominions Office, which suggested that the cabinet should supply arms and provide the guarantee to respect Irish neutrality. But while the cabinet agreed to the arms proposal, it rejected the other suggestion.

In the coming weeks the British turned over some

weapons — including 20,000 American rifles. In a deliberate effort to get the Irish to realise that they were dependent on Britain rather than America for security, Roosevelt had given the rifles to the British so that they could get the credit for turning them over to Ireland. The British gesture then had the effect of relieving much of the Irish anxiety about British intentions, at least until after the American elections.

On election day in the United States, however, Churchill gave vent to his frustration at Dublin's refusal to allow Britain to use Irish ports. He told the House of Commons that the denial of Irish facilities was 'a most heavy and grievous burden and one which should never have been placed on our shoulders, broad though they be.'

The speech received extensive coverage in the American press. The prestigeous *New York Times* reported it on its front page alongside news of Roosevelt's re-election, and the influential New York *Herald Tribune's* military affairs correspondent — who described Britain's inability to use Irish bases as 'a serious handicap' — suggested that 'American opinion, highly regarded always in Ireland, might well be of some service in urging a change of attitude at Dublin.'[16]

De Valera was deeply troubled by the prominence that the press gave to Churchill's speech. 'I was prepared to take it, as a simple, perhaps natural, expression of regret,' he said. 'I would have refrained from making any comment upon it were it not that it has been followed by an extensive press campaign in Britain itself, and re-echoed in the United States of America.'[17]

The attitude of the American Minister, David Gray, who had taken over from Cudahy in April, must have been particularly disturbing to the Taoiseach. Two days after Churchill's speech, for example, Gray told Joseph Walshe that the Irish government should 'be prepared for support of Great Britain in the American press in case Churchill, moved by what he conceived to be a necessity, announced that he would occupy the ports by force.'[18]

That afternoon de Valera went before the Dáil and re-iterated his determination to remain neutral. 'Any attempt to bring pressure to bear on us by any side,' he said, 'could only lead to bloodshed.' He again made it clear that Ireland would invite the help of any invader's enemy.[19]

The Taoiseach later admitted that he realised that while there would have neen no difficulty in securing British help in the event of a German invasion, 'it would not have been so easy to get other forces against the British if they had attacked us.'[20] Consequently the only real protection that the Irish had against Britain was American public opinion, with the result that if Americans could be convinced that Britain had a right to take Irish bases, then the Irish government would have only its own meagre resources with which to resist.

De Valera therefore sought to bolster his American support by sending an open telegram to the President of AARIR asking the association and all friends of Ireland to organise and put the Irish case clearly before the American public. Explaining that it would be 'an inhuman outrage' to force Ireland into the war when the country was virtually defenceless, he contended that the Irish people had the same right as Americans to keep out of the war, and were determined to 'defend that right to the utmost.'[21] In another obvious appeal to American opinon little over a week later, he gave a United Press correspondent an interview in which he stressed his inability to give bases to Britain without becoming implicated in the conflict.

'If we handed over the ports to Britain,' the Taoiseach explained, 'we would thereby involve ourselves directly in the war, with all its consequences. You have seen what has happened to London, notwithstanding its defences. Ireland is not a nation which can spend ten million pounds a day on armaments and if London is suffering as it is what would happen to Dublin, Cork, and other Irish cities relatively unprotected. If we were attacked, we should no doubt have to face those dangers, but no nation can be asked to court them.'[22]

The response in the United States was swift, as the Irish-American ethnic press denounced Churchill's speech, lauded de Valera's reply, and called for American support for Irish neutrality. An editorial from the Irish-American owned *New York Enquirer,* accusing Churchill of talking like Hitler and being 'eager to commit the crowning blunder of his career by making an assault on Ireland,' was inserted into the *Congressional Record,* and a copy of the editorial, along with a goodwill message signed by eighty senators, one hundred and eighty-eight members of the House of Representatives, and nineteen governors was sent to de Valera.[23] Such a gesture could not be dismissed lightly, especially as Roosevelt's efforts to aid Britain were dependent on Congressional support.

De Valera's appeal for organised American support for Irish neutrality was given a very sympathetic hearing in New York, where the American Friends of Irish Neutrality was established under the chairmanship of an Irish-born lawyer, Paul O'Dwyer. That organisation soon began establishing chapters in Irish-American centres throughout the country.[24]

Both of the Allied and American representatives in Dublin believed that Churchill's obvious attempt to exert public pressure on de Valera was a mistake. John H. Kelly, the Canadian High Commissioner, warned his government that a propaganda campaign could 'do no good and may prove detrimental.'[25] The American Minister was confident that de Valera, whom he considered as 'probably the most adroit politician in Europe', would not be browbeaten into submission. 'He has the qualities of martyr, fanatic and Machiavelli,' Gray wrote. 'No one can outwit him, frighten or blandish him. Remember that he is not pro-German nor personally anti-British but only pro-de Valera. My view is that he will do business on his own terms or must be overcome by force.'[26]

The British Representative warned the Dominions Office against a propaganda campaign. Prior to the revival of the ports issue, he noted that Irish sentiment towards Britain had been steadily improving but there was a danger that the Taoiseach, who was in a 'very agitated and bitter mood' could undermine all the progress. Maffey warned that de Valera might 'exploit at once all the resources of the old tribal hatred. Whatever Mr de Valera may be in Geneva, here, in Ireland, he has never in essentials moved from the trace he has consistently followed — the narrow avenue of hate.' The British Representative therefore asked for persmission to assure de Valera that Britain would respect Irish neutrality,[27] but Churchill had just refused to authorise such an assurance. 'I think it would be better to let de Valera stew in his own juice for a while,' he wrote to the Dominions Secretary. The Prime Minister added that Maffey 'should not be encouraged to think that his only task is to mollify de Valera and make everything, including our ruin, pass off pleasantly. Apart from this, the less we say to de Valera at this juncture the better, and certainly nothing must be said to reassure him.'[28]

Dublin was actually able to use the rather minatory British attitude to its own advantage in relations with Germany. Basically the Irish approach had been to try to convince the Germans that it was to their advantage not to violate Irish neutrality. And this task was undoubtedly simplified with the British clamouring for the use of Irish ports — the denial of which seemed to favour Germany. By playing on the British pressure during the summer de Valera had been able to secure the German promise to respect Irish neutrality. Nevertheless he left as many contacts as possible with the German Minister to Joseph Walshe and his assistant at the department of External Affairs, Frederick H. Boland.

In conversations with the German Minister, Walshe and Boland emphasised in subtle ways how Irish policy was working to the advantage of the Germans. When it looked liked Hitler was in an unbeatable position following the fall of France, for example, Walshe expressed the hope to Hempel that Germany would not abandon Ireland to the British.[29] He was in effect contending that the country's neutrality had been so favourable to Germany that Irish authorities were afraid that the British might use Dublin as their scapegoat for losing the war, and might retaliate against Ireland after the conflict unless the Germans were willing to protect her. On another occasion, following a meeting with Walshe, Hempel reported that the 'Irish government apparently believes that if the Irish element in the United States is properly used, it could constitute a powerful influence in our favour, likewise the Irish-American press.'[30] The Irishman was not necessarily advocating that the Germans should try to manipulate anglophobic elements among the Irish-Americans. In fact, he actually warned that any German political intervention in the United States might do more harm than good. His remarks therefore could be seen as a way of persuading the German Minister that Irish-Americans would be acting to Germany's advantage so long as Berlin did not antagonise them by violating Irish sovereignty. Nevertheless there could be little doubt that Walshe was also trying to ingratiate himself with the Axis representatives by appearing friendly to their interests.[31]

He was undoubtedly trying to give the impression to the Axis representatives that he sympathised with them. American intelligence later learned from an 'entirely reliable' source, for example, that Walshe had told the Italian Minister that while Ireland was not in imminent danger of a British attack, her position would be seriously weakened if the United States entered the war, which was appearing increasingly likely at the time. The Irishman therefore advised that the decisive Axis attack on Britain should not be delayed too long.[32]

The Americans were deeply suspicious of Walshe, and those suspicions could only have been strengthened by some critical reports from Gray, whose information was not always reliable. In fact, he tended to have some most unconventional sources. On once occasion, for instance, he sent President Roosevelt transcripts of what he believed were messages from the late Arthur Balfour to the effect that Walshe was 'hand in glove with the German Minister.' A believer in spiritualism, Gray wrote that the former British Prime Minister, who had died more than a decade earlier, had informed him during a seance that Walshe was 'the leading Quisling' among some well-organised fifth columnists.[33]

Notwithstanding the uneasiness that Walshe was causing in Allied circles, his attempt to depict Irish neutrality as advantageous to Germany did simplify efforts to keep the Germans in line. During the summer of 1940, for example, the Department of External Affairs contended that German attacks on clearly marked Irish ships, especially within Irish territorial waters, were endangering neutrality because the British could cite such attacks to contend that Ireland could not defend herself, which could, in turn, be used to justify Britain seizing Irish bases to prevent Germany getting hold of them. Hempel therefore advised Berlin to try to avoid Irish shipping, especially when the ships were away from British ports.

In December 1940 the Irish again utilised the British threat to their own advantage — this time to stall efforts to increase the size of the German legation in Dublin. Irish authorities used the excuse that there were grave difficulties in arranging transportation for the additional staff. Boland explained to Hempel that Dublin feared possible reaction in both Britain and the United States if a German plane were suddenly allowed to land in Ireland. He said that it might weaken American support for Irish neutrality.

When the German Minister insisted on making arrangements for additional staff, Walshe told him that de Valera feared that the move might be cited by the British as grounds for alleging that Ireland was being used for German espionage, or even that they might conclude that there was some kind of German-Irish plot, as they had during the First World War. But Hempel remained unpersuaded. He maintained that Germany had a right to acquire additional staff for the legation, so a meeting was arranged for him with de Valera.

The Taoiseach was in a thorny spot. The Germans were unquestionably entitled to extra staff, if only to replace one of their men who had recently died in Ireland. De Valera therefore agreed to the request but, in view of the need to avoid giving Britain any pretext for invading Ireland, he insisted that unorthodox methods of transportation, such as an unscheduled flight or a parachute drop, could not be used. The new staff members would have to arrive by the normal commercial route. It was only afterwards that Hempel learned to his dismay that all ships and aircraft bound for Ireland stopped in Britain, which of course forced the Germans to abandon their planned staff increase. As a result, in spite of rumours that there were as many as a hundred people on the legation staff, it never consisted of more than half a dozen at any stage of the war.

No sooner had de Valera coped with the danger posed by the efforts to increase the size of the German legation than he was faced with a far graver crisis as there were unmistakable signs that the British were beginning to exert economic pressure on Ireland. Terry de Valera, the Taoiseach's youngest son, later contended that his father actually feared a British attack at the time, but there was really little danger of it. The British only planned to use economic measures and the cabinet had decided that even those should 'not be allowed to clash' with President Roosevelt's efforts to secure Congressional authorisation for lend-lease.[34]

Realising that the country did not have nearly enough ships to cater for her own needs, the Taoiseach turned to the United States for help. But as Gray and the State Department had already made it clear that they supported Britain staunchly, there was little use in appealing to the Roosevelt administration, so de Valera appealed directly to the American people. In a Christmas address to the United States, which was broadcast over the Columbia Broadcasting System (CBS), he called on the Americans to sell Ireland arms and also ships, which were needed to transport food because the country was facing serious shortages as a result of a blockade by the belligerents. 'I know,' he said, 'it will be hard for you to realise that there is at this moment probably no country in Europe so effectively blockaded as we are.'

Since Britain was in control of the seas around Ireland, it seemed that de Valera was accusing the British of blockading Ireland. And that impression was strengthened when CBS released what was purported to be the text of the speech because, in justifying the need for arms, he was attributed with having said that the 'overshadowing anxiety' of his government was that the Irish people would once more be forced 'to battle against Britain and the British.'[35] Although de Valera had not in fact mentioned either Britain or the British by name, CBS initially stood by its text, and it was not until some days later that it corrected the version.[36]

American officials resented de Valera's address, because it fitted neatly into the propaganda of those opposing Roosevelt's efforts to increase American aid for Britain, in addition to being a blatant appeal to the American people over the head of their government. Gray protested to the Taoiseach personally that the speech 'appeared to be an attempt to put the pressure of the Irish-American vote on the government.'[37] Instead of speaking directly to the American people, Gray suggested that an emissary should be sent to Washington to explain Irish difficulties.

At the time those difficulties were indeed formidable because events seemed to be closing in on the Dublin government from various quarters. For example, the need for arms became particularly obvious in the first three days of the new year when some apparently disorientated German planes bombed scattered Irish localities. About the same time in London, the British cabinet formally decided to exert economic pressure by cutting off the export of certain specified items and cutting down on coal and fuel supplies to Ireland.

When the Irish protested that the move was contrary to an informal understanding arrived at between the two countries after Dublin turned over the seven modern oil tankers and agreed not to compete with Britain in chartering neutral ships, the British replied that as there had been no formal agreement, they were acting within their rights in simply terminating the understanding. Henceforth the Irish would be free to charter neutral ships, but of course by then Britain had much of the neutral shipping under contract. As a result the British estimated that Ireland would at best be able to charter only enough ships to fulfil about a quarter of her needs.

Churchill had been the driving inspiration behind the economic pressure. He was simply not prepared to tolerate a situation in which Britain was willingly supplying the Irish while the latter were refusing to provide the help that he thought Britain needed. Or, as he explained when asking if Roosevelt had any objections to the cut-back of British supplies for Ireland, why should Britain continue to supply the Irish 'when de Valera is quite content to sit happy and see us strangle.'[38]

Although the Roosevelt administration raised no objections, Churchill was obviously thinking of American public opinion when he suggested that the coercive designs of the economic policy should be carefully concealed. He told the cabinet that 'it should be emphasised that this step was taken in no vindictive spirit and only dire necessity had forced us into such a step.' The cabinet then decided that the Ministry of Information should inform the press that 'the Government viewed this measure with profound regret.'[39]

As things stood American public opinion was already so favourable towards Britain that it soon became questionable whether Dublin could really depend on it as a deterrant to a British violation of Irish neutrality. This became particularly apparent early in the new year with the publication of a Gallup poll showing that sixty-three per cent of Americans thought that Britain should be allowed to use Irish ports, while only sixteeen per cent opposed the proposition, with the remainder undecided. Only a bare majority of fifty-two per cent of Americans whose fathers were born in Ireland supported the stand taken by the Irish government, while forty per cent actually thought that the ports should be handed over to the British.

After the publication of the poll, Maffey found the Taoiseach 'more uneasy today than he had ever been at any stage of his non-stop political career.' Previously de Valera had been able to use 'Irish fanaticism on a bigger stage. But it is the soul of England which stirs the world today,' the British Representative observed, 'and Éire is a bog with a petty leader raking over old muck heaps. He has in the past enjoyed world prestige; he is vain and ambitious but the track he has followed without looking either to right or to left is now leading into insignificance.' De Valera was obviously worried by the trend of American opinion. 'These Irish-Americans are the pillars of Mr de Valera's temple,' Maffey explained. 'They created him, preserved him, and endowed him.'[40]

Some of Maffey's virulence was undoubtedly designed as a sop for Churchill, who tended to believe that the British Representative was too soft on de Valera. Thus by criticising the Irish leader in such harsh terms, Maffey could hope that Churchill might at least seriously consider his suggestions.

During the meeting about which the British Representative was reporting, de Valera had actually given permission for British planes to fly in an air corridor over County Donegal, but had gone on to criticise British policy towards Ireland as being 'stupid'. In recent months, he warned, Irish authorities had come to fear Britain as much as Germany, with the result that if the Nazis invaded, 'they might not meet the spirited opposition' that they would have met six months earlier. 'Mr de Valera is telling the truth when he says that if we arm Éire we shall create a most powerful weapon against a German invasion and establish a good friend on our flank,' wrote Maffey, who therefore desired that Churchill's hardline policy should be reconsidered, with at least an assurance being given to de Valera that Britain would respect Irish sovereignty.

Churchill, who only a fortnight earlier had told the Dominions Office that Britain would seize Irish bases if their denial should 'threaten to become mortal', was again unwilling to accept Maffey's advice. 'I could in no circumstances give the guarantee asked for,' the Prime Minister wrote. He was also reluctant to provide any further arms unless the Irish were first prepared to make definite preparations to join the Allies. 'Until we are so satisfied,' Churchill added, 'we do not wish them to have further arms, and certainly will not give them ourselves.'[41]

In view of Churchill's attitude, de Valera was really left with little alternative but to try to bolster his flagging American support. He therefore decided to send Frank Aiken, the Minister for the Co-ordination of Defensive Measures, as an emissary to the United States.

The Taoiseach told the American people of the mission in his annual St Patrick's Day address to the United States. During the speech he said that Ireland was suffering from 'serious shortages' as a result of a blockade by both sides in the war. In trying to blockade each other, he explained, the belligerents were blockading Ireland, so he was therefore asking the American people to facilitate Aiken's efforts to purchase ships with which Ireland could supply her own needs, and arms to protect the country against invasion. This reiteration of the charge first made in his Christmas address that both sides were blockading Ireland again played into the hands of anglophobic elements opposed to Roosevelt's foreign policy, with the result that the speech created a most unfavourable climate for the Aiken mission.

Although Aiken was subsequently accorded the courtesy of a hearing by all leading officials of the Roosevelt administration, he was unable to make progress with them. His meeting with Roosevelt was particularly unsatisfactory. The American President refused to believe that Ireland was in any danger of being attacked by Britain, and when Aiken brazenly maintained that the threat of such an attack was very real, Roosevelt lost his temper. 'I have never heard of anything so preposterous in all my life,' the frustrated President said as he jerked a table cloth from in front of him, sending cutlery flying and ending what had been a most unsatisfactory interview.[42]

Once it became apparent that Aiken would not be able to make progress with the Roosevelt administration, he went to Irish-American centres and appealed directly for American support. He travelled from coast to coast and associated with some of Roosevelt's bitterest critics — among them men like Charles A. Lindbergh, John T. Flynn, David I. Walsh, Burton K. Wheeler, and even John Cudahy, the former Minister to Ireland who had only just returned from Berlin where he had personally tried to enlist the help of Hitler himself in an attempt to prevent what he saw as Roosevelt's drift towards American involvement in the war.

Yielding to Irish-America pressure, Roosevelt offered to sell two ships and give $500,000 worth of Red Cross supplies to Ireland, but he declined to furnish arms. He said that American weapons could only be spared for those nations 'actively waging war on behalf of the maintenance of Democracy.'

'I'd hate like hell to think our nuisance value was only half a million dollars,' Aiken remarked bitterly after the President's announcement.[43] Not only had the Irish emissary undoubtedly made a nuisance of himself in the eyes of the Roosevelt administration, but his remark seemed to indicate that he had done so deliberately. Hence it should have been of little surprise that relations between Dublin and Washington were strained for some time.

The end of the Aiken mission actually co-incided with the German invasion of the Soviet Union which relieved much of the Irish apprehension caused not only by the danger of a German invasion, but also by the threat of a British attack. It would afterwards be possible to look back and realise that as of the end of June 1941, Ireland had successfully weathered what was for her the worst of the storm.

When the United States entered the war following the attack on Pearl Harbour almost six months later, de Valera offered his sympathy to the Americans, but he emphasised that Irish policy was going to remain unchanged. 'We can only be a friendly neutral,' he said. From the moment the war began, neutrality was the only policy open to the government. 'Any other policy,' he explained, 'would have divided our people, and for a divided nation to fling itself into this war would be to commit suicide.'[44]

John D. Kearney, who had taken over as Canadian High Commissioner some months earlier, had no doubts about the Taoiseach's sincerity. 'It has been demonstrated,' he reported, 'that the Irish government will do almost anything to help us short of involving themselves in the war.'[45]

In the following months de Valera continued to demonstrate the benevolence of his policy towards the Allies. Hundreds of Allied airmen who came down in Ireland were spirited across the border into Northern Ireland, including General Jacob Devers, the Commander of United States forces in Europe, whose plane crashed near Athy. When the Americans suggested that the Irish government should agree not to intern Allied pilots who came down in Ireland while on non-operational flights, such as training missions or while testing equipment, the Irish agreed to the proposal, but in practice they never bothered to check on the non-operational claims.

'Under the circumstances,' Kearney noted, 'the meaning of the words "non-operational flight" has sometimes been stretched almost beyond recognition.'[46] He even managed to persuade de Valera to apply the non-operational theory retroactively so that all but eight of the thirty-two Allied airmen then interned were released in October 1943. The remainder were secretly freed following the Allied invasion of Europe in June 1944.

One man who was not impressed by de Valera's benevolence towards the Allies was David Gray. He was one of those people who felt that those who were not prepared to join the Allies, were therefore against them. 'This was his stern unshakeable principle,' according to Maffey. 'In his diplomacy there was no room for compromise.'[47]

The American Minister made such a nuisance of himself even before the United States entered the war that Walshe informally asked the Canadian High Commissioner in October 1941 to use his influence to have him recalled, but the Canadians refused to become involved, although the Department of External Affairs in Ottawa was certainly not impressed with Gray's credentials. Oscar D. Skelton, the secretary of the department, described him as 'a former newspaperman, with not much fame,' whose main accomplishment was to have married Eleanor Roosevelt's aunt.[48] Obviously Gray owed his appointment to that family relationship, so de Valera was reluctant to demand his recall for fear of complicating relations with the White House. Nevertheless the Irish eventually became so exasperated, after the State Department demanded an explanation for a ridiculous rumour about the presence of hundreds of Japanese tourists in Ireland, where there were actually only four Japanese people, that Robert Brennan, the Irish Minister to the United States, suggested in a note to the State Department that a new minister should be appointed who would be 'an independent and unprejudiced witness to seek and make known the truth.' The approach was resented in Washington, and the note was returned to Brennan as 'offensive in the extreme'. Thus the

Irish were stuck with Gray.[49]

The latter was dissatisfied because he believed that Irish neutrality hurt the Allied war effort in two ways — by denying needed bases and by affording Axis diplomats a chance to spy on the Allies. Although the Irish had for long been contending that Irish bases would be of little use to the Allies, none of the Allied representatives in Dublin believed that argument.

In January 1943 when the Germans launched a U-boat offensive in the Atlantic, the British and Canadian representatives thought that there might be an opportunity of securing facilities if the United States asked for them. Gray liked the idea, so Maffey went over to London to discuss the proposal with his government. Although the U-boat campaign was at its height while he was in Britain, Maffey found that there was little support for the idea of asking for Irish ports. Deputy Prime Minister Clement Attlee explained that defending the facilities would 'probably' be more trouble than they were worth.[50]

When Gray broached authorities in Washington, he was met with basically the same objection. The chiefs of staff explained that as long as Germany controlled the French coast, Allied shipping had to use the route via Northern Ireland, where the Allies already had facilities. The chiefs of staff were therefore opposed to asking for Irish bases because they feared that such facilities would only hamper the war effort by obliging the Allies to defend them. Thus it became apparent that both Gray and Churchill had greatly overestimated the strategic value of the Irish ports, the denial of which — far from hampering the Allied war effort — actually enhanced it.

The possibility of the Axis diplomats spying, on the other hand, was a different proposition. They undoubtedly did pose an espionage threat to the Allies. In August 1942, for example, Hempel had managed to warn Berlin that Canadian troops were massing in the south of England for an apparent landing on the French coast.[51] There followed shortly afterwards the disastrous landing at Dieppe.

The Dublin government did take steps to try to prevent the German legation from engaging in espionage. On several occasions it demanded that the Germans stop using their radio transmitter — going so far as threatening to confiscate the equipment. Finally in December 1943 after the British informally requested that Irish authorities remove the transmitter, Hempel was compelled to deposit it in the vault of a Dublin bank, from where he could withdraw it only with the approval of the Irish Department of External Affairs.

Having complied with informal Allied requests not only concerning the German transmitter but also numerous other matters over the years, de Valera was stunned when, without warning less than two months later, Gray delivered a formal note from the United States government demanding the expulsion of German and Japanese representatives from Ireland on the grounds that they were an espionage threat to Allied preparations for the forthcoming invasion of Europe.[52]

'Of course our answer will be no,' de Valera said before he had even finished reading the note. 'As long as I am here it will be no.'

'We have done everything to prevent Axis espionage,' he added on completing the document, 'going beyond what we might reasonably be expected to do and I am satisfied that there are no leaks from this country; for a year and a half you have been advertisng the invasion of Europe and what has got out about it has not been from Éire; the German Minister, I am satisfied, has behaved very correctly and decently and as a neutral we will not send him away.'[53]

Next day when Maffey delivered a British note supporting the American request, de Valera became angry. He was annoyed that in spite of the informal working relationship that had existed, the Allies had deliverd formal notes without making any informal representations beforehand. The Taoiseach contended that the move was an effort to push him into the war and thus deprive Ireland of the symbol of her independence. 'It was obvious,' Maffey reported, 'that he attached immense importance to this symbolic factor.'[54]

The Irish army was put on alert, and there was a great deal of public uneasiness, which could only have been exacerbated by de Valera announcing that it was 'a time of extreme danger' in which defence forces should be prepared. 'No words which I can use,' he said, 'would be strong enough to express my conviction of the necessity of maintaining these forces at their maximum strength and efficiency.'[55]

Wild rumours abounded. There were reports that the Allies had invaded from Northern Ireland and that there were battleships off the Dublin coast. There were even rumours that some members of the Irish opposition had been arrested and shot.

Having unsuccessfully tried to get the Canadians to use their influence to have the notes withdrawn, de Valera had his formal rejection delivered to the Americans on 7 March 1944. Although it had been agreed by all concerned that the notes should be kept secret, the story broke and the State Department then released the texts.

The whole affair created a wave of hysteria in the American press, which accused de Valera of helping the Germans and even the Japanese, and thereby endangering the lives of hundreds of thousands of American boys. 'The case demands action,' one editorial declared. 'Either Éire throws out the Jap and German spies or stands the consequences. Whether blockade or more extreme measures will be necessary to bring Prime Minister de Valera to face realities is for him to decide.'[56] A public opinion survey conducted in mid-March 1944 found that two-thirds of the seventy-one per cent of Americans who were aware of the affair felt that the United States should take further action. Of those people, thirty-eight per cent recommended trade sanctions, while thirty-five per cent thought that a degree of force should be used, with some people actually advocating that war be declared on Ireland.

Although the presence of Axis representatives in Ireland did undoubtedly provide grounds for Allied caution, if not concern, it should be emphasised that the presentation of the formal notes was not motivated primarily by security fears but by political considerations, which will be discussed at greater length in the next chapter. The whole affair had been designed to wreck de Valera's public standing in the United States so that he would not be able to inject the partition issue into post-war American politics.

While the publicity severely damaged de Valera's image in the United States, his popularity soared in Ireland. This became particularly evident in May 1944 when he called a surprise general election and his party was returned with a fourteen seat majority. The editor of the *Irish Times* observed that he had the American note to thank for the victory because it had given him the opportunity to demonstrate Ireland's 'absolute independence of everybody, including on this occasion the United States and to figure in the eyes of his own followers as one of the greatest statesmen since Abraham Lincoln.'[57]

De Valera also used neutrality to further demonstrate Ireland's independence during the final months of the war by taking an independent, though somewhat equivocal stand when the Americans asked for a guarantee that Dublin would not grant asylum to Nazi war criminals. 'The Irish government,' he explained, 'can give no assurance which would preclude them from exercising that right should justice, charity or honour or the interest of the nation so require.' But he then went on to indicate that there was no intention of altering the long-observed practice of denying 'admission to all aliens whose presence would be at variance with the policy of neutrality, or detrimental to the Irish people, or inconsistent with the desire of the Irish people to avoid injury to the interests of friendly states.'[58] In other words the Irish government would not guarantee that it would not grant political asylum to war criminals, although it had no intention of doing so.

On 30 April 1945 the American Minister came to de Valera with another request. This time he wanted permission to seize the German legation in Dublin before Hempel would have time to destroy documents. Reading from a memorandum, Gray noted that Allied forces were almost in total control of Germany and that Ireland had, in effect, recognised the collapse of the Berlin government by withdrawing the Irish *chargé d'affaires* to safety in Switzerland. As title to all the German government's property would be vested in the Allies once the defeat had been finalised, the

American Minister asked that the United States be allowed to take possession of the German legation immediately in order to get hold of secret codes before the staff there could destroy them. He explained that the codes could be used to save the lives and property of Irish nationals as well as others in the event that after the surrender some sub-marines tried to carry on the struggle, or if there were armed pockets of resistance.

'As I proceeded,' Gray reported, 'Mr de Valera grew red and looked very sour. He was evidently annoyed, but his manner was correct. When I finished, he slapped the copy of the memorandum, which I had presented to him, on his desk and said, "This is a matter for my legal advisers. It is not a matter that I can discuss with you now."'[59]

Gray argued that time was of the essence, but de Valera refused to discuss the matter further.

Next day Walshe informed the American Minister that Hempel would be instructed to hand over his keys once the surrender had been announced, and that the Americans could then, and only then, take charge of the legation. It was obvious that they were not going to have to wait very long as there were reports that day that Hitler had killed himself.

Hitler's death led to a defiant gesture of Irish independence that caused a sensation of shock and revulsion when the Taoiseach went to the German Legation to express his condolence to Hempel. The actions set off a firestorm of criticism not only in Britain, but right across the United States and Canada.

Sir Robert Vansittart, the British diplomat, described de Valera's gesture as 'the silliest act of the whole war'.[60] That the Taoiseach had only observed the strict protocol of a neutral state did not matter. 'Considering the character and the record of the man for whose death he was expressing grief,' the *New York Times* declared, 'there is obviously something wrong with the protocol, the neutrality, or Mr de Valera.'[61]

Although the criticism was not reflected in the heavily censored Irish newspapers, the Canadian High Commissioner reported that 'nothing which Mr de Valera has done during the years which I have been in Dublin has evoked such widespread criticism and much of it came from persons who are normally supporters of his own party.'[62]

The Taoiseach did not try to account for his actions publicly, but he did explain privately that it would have been an 'unpardonable discourtesy to the German nation and to Dr Hempel himself' if he had not offered his condolence.[63] Yet there could be no doubt that his annoyance with Gray had also played a part in the gesture. Less than three weeks earlier, following the death of President Roosevelt, de Valera had paid what the American Minister himself described 'as a very moving tribute' in the Dáil, which then adjourned as a mark of respect. 'I thought I knew this country and its people,' Gray wrote to the President's widow next day, 'but this was something new. There was a great deal of genuine feeling.'[64] Consequently it would have been insulting to the German Minister if the death of his leader had simply been ignored. And the Taoiseach was not about to insult Hempel for whom he had a much higher regard than for the American Minister.

'During the whole of the war,' de Valera wrote, 'Dr Hempel's conduct was irreproachable. He was always and invariably correct — in marked contrast with Gray. I certainly was not going to add to his humiliation in the hour of defeat.'[65]

Following the conclusion of hostilities in Europe the press censorship was lifted in Ireland, and the Taoiseach's action in regard to Hitler's death appeared in an even poorer light as the Irish people were finally confronted with the real magnitude of Nazi tyranny. Then Churchill afforded the Taoiseach an opportunity of redeeming himself completely in the eyes of the Irish public.

On 13 May 1945 in the course of a victory address, the British Prime Minister made a strong attack on Irish neutrality. Although some people thought the remarks were prompted by annoyance over de Valera's actions eleven days earlier, it was more probable that these were a calculated move to bolster support for Northern Ireland in the event that Dublin sought to revive the partition issue. In the speech, for example, Churchill described the denial of

Irish bases as 'a deadly blow in our life and if it had not been for the loyalty and friendship of Northern Ireland we should have been forced to come to close quarters with Mr de Valera or perish for ever from the earth.' He added that Britain simply 'left the de Valera government to frolic with the Germans and later with the Japanese representatives to their hearts' content.'

There was a great air of anticipation in Ireland as people waited for de Valera to respond. It was confidently expected that he would deliver a broadside at the British leader, possibly evoking all the old anglophobic hatreds of the Irish people. But the Taoiseach responded with a reasoned statesmanlike speech that won admiration throughout Ireland and quickly overcame the domestic resentment over his condolence gesture following Hitler's death.

De Valera's speech, which was carried live on Radio Éireann on 16 May 1945, was probably the best and most effective speech of his long career. He began by thanking God for sparing Ireland from the conflagration that had left much of Europe in ruins. Next he expressed gratitude to the various groups that had contributed towards the success of the country's neutrality. And only then did he refer to Churchill's remarks.

The Taoiseach explained that he knew what people were expecting him to say, and what he would have said a quarter of a century earlier. But the occasion demanded something else, he added somewhat condescendingly, because Churchill could be excused for being carried away in the flush of victory, while there would be no such excuse for himself. Speaking calmly de Valera said:

Mr Churchill makes it clear that, in certain circumstances, he would have violated our neutrality and that he would justify his action by Britain's necessity. It seems strange to me that Mr Churchill does not see that this, if it be accepted, would mean that Britain's necessity would become a moral code and that, when this necessity became sufficiently great, other people's rights were not to count. It is quite true that other great powers believe in this same code — in their own regard — and have behaved in accordance with it. That is precisely why we have the disastrous succession of wars — World War No. 1 and World War No. 2 — and shall it be World War No. 3?

He then turned to praise Churchill for resisting the temptation to violate Irish neutrality:

> It is, indeed, hard for the strong to be just to the weak. But acting justly always has its rewards. By resisting his temptation in this instance, Mr Churchill, instead of adding another horrid chapter to the already blood-stained record of the relations between England and this country, has advanced the cause of international morality an important step. . .

The Taoiseach next mentioned how partition had poisoned Anglo-Irish relations, and he intimated that this had made it impossible for Ireland to do anything other than remain neutral. He then reached the emotional crescendo of his reply to the British leader:

> Mr Churchill is proud of Britain's stand alone, after France had fallen and before America entered the war. Could he not find in his heart the generosity to acknowledge that there is a small nation that stood alone, not for one year or two, but for several hundred years against aggression; that endured spoilations, famines, massacres in endless succession; that was clubbed many times into insensibility, but that each time on returning to consciousness, took up the fight anew; a small nation that could never be got to accept defeat and has never surrendered her soul?

The public reaction to the address was overwhelming. 'With little exception,' the Canadian representative reported, 'Mr de Valera's broadcast is regarded in Ireland as a masterpiece, and it is looked upon as probably his best effort. It has served to almost still the criticism which his visit to the German Minister provoked, and, in so far as I can judge, on balance, Mr de Valera now stands in higher favour in Ireland than he did before his visit to the German Minister.'[66]

Although the war had ended there were still some loose ends to be cleared up in regards to Irish neutrality. De Valera absolutely refused to turn over Hempel to the Allies, and he demanded a guarantee that none of the two hundred and fifty Germans that had been interned in Ireland would be handed over to the Russians. Although Gray objected strenuously that agreeing to such a condition would involve discriminating against an ally, Britain gave the desired assurance, and scrupulously complied with it when almost all of the internees were turned over.

Initially the Irish leader also refused to turn over the German spies who had been captured in Ireland. Later he did have a change of heart on the question, but this led to some friction within his cabinet as Gerald Boland, the Minister for Justice, became bitterly resentful on learning that the Department of External Affairs had agreed to hand over the former spies. He was particularly critical of the decision to deport Herman Goertz, who was threatening to commit suicide rather than return to Germany, where he was afraid of being persecuted by communists because he had been involved in suppressing the Sparticist Revolt in 1918. Boland actually tendered his resignation over the deportation decision, but de Valera persuaded him to withdraw it on giving him authority to deal with the issue.[67]

Boland then tried to persuade the British and Americans to allow Goertz to stay in Ireland. When this failed, Goertz was taken into custody in May 1947 and was told that he was definitely being deported. He then carried out his threat and killed himself.

Irish authorities quickly rescinded the deportation order on another of the Germans, Werner Unland. He and his British-born wife had both threatened to kill themselves, if they were deported. When it became clear that the Irish would ignore Allied protests on the issue, the British agreed to drop their demand for Unland on certain conditions, but Gray was apparently not told about the matter.[68] When he resigned on 30 June 1947, he thought that all the Germans had been handed over. The loose ends of Ireland's wartime neutrality were quietly cleared up.

CHAPTER FIVE

Unfinished Business

The Anti-Partition Campaign

For all practical purposes Irish neutrality conclusively demonstrated that the Twenty-six Counties were a completely independent political entity. Consequently there remained only the ending of partition for de Valera to realise his dream of complete national independence. And there could be little doubt that he planned to wage a campaign to achieve the realisation of this dream once the war had ended and the international situation was quiet enough for Dublin to exploit Ireland's traditional support overseas.

Prior to the war de Valera had clearly indicated that he intended to wage an international propaganda campaign to bring about Irish unity. He had arranged a tour of the United States which he admitted was primarily aimed at enlisting American public support for the ending of partition, but of course the tour was cancelled with the outbreak of the Second World War. While admitting that 'it was quite clear we could not make much progress' towards unity during the war, he later stated that his government nevertheless did everything possible to highlight the issue.[1]

In his St Patrick's Day address to the United States in 1940, for example, he delivered an emotional denunciation of partition. 'After an existance for thousands of years as one natural national unit,' he told his American audience, 'our territory was divided twenty years ago by a British Act of Parliament.' Describing that division as 'absurd' and having 'no justification in politics, religion, geography or economics,' he said that it had been brought about simply because the British parliament 'considered that its own interests would be better served by it.' In attempting to maintain it, he accused the British of a 'succession of devises' such as gerrymandering constituencies and using a franchise system in local elections that allowed unionists to elect a majority of representatives to local councils even in areas where they actually constituted a minority. 'The ordinary principles of democracy have been inverted as majorities turned into minorities,' de Valera said, 'so that a pretence may be made of government with the consent of the governed.' He went on to contend that Britain herself was being damaged by partition. 'An Ireland partitioned must always be a reproach,' he said, 'lessening her moral influence throughout the world and always causing the sincerity of her motives to be questioned.'

Throughout the war de Valera used the partition issue to justify Irish neutrality in order to enable Ireland to retain much of her traditional sympathy among Irish-Americans, especially after the United States entered the war, when the partition grievance provided virtually the only context in which Irish-Americans could understand Irish neutrality. The retention of Irish-American sympathy was vital during the war because it was virtually the only thing that the Taoiseach could use to compel Churchill to keep his hands off Irish bases and not violate the neutrality that the British leader so obviously despised.

There could be little doubt that de Valera was firmly convinced that the existence of partition left him with no real alternative but to pursue neutrality. Even Gray, who was one of the bitterest critics of neutrality, observed that the Taoiseach was inspired by neither fear nor hate 'but chiefly by a haunting dread of repeating the tragedy of 1922.'[2] But it became evident that the partition issue did not provide the prime motivation for his policy when he refused to consider the idea of bargaining with neutrality in return for unity. In April 1940, for instance, before the German offensive in the west had really begun, Gray asked the Taoiseach about the possibility of breaking off diplomatic relations with Germany and allowing Britain to use the port of Berehaven in return for Irish unity, but the proposal was flatly rejected. 'We could never bargain with our neutrality,' de Valera explained.[3]

Later, after the German invasion of the Low Countries, Gray again brought up the possibility of bargaining with neutrality in return for unity, but was met with essentially the same reply, as the Taoiseach told him 'with some heat' that 'the neutrality of Ireland was not for sale.'[4]

Although de Valera had convinced the British that his government would conclude an alliance with them in return for the ending of partition before the war, he warned them that it would be too late to conclude such an arrangement once the conflict had begun. Yet London still thought that he might be willing to make a deal. When the fall of France became imminent, Irish bases seemed to take on added significance, so the British government decided to approach the Taoiseach. Hence Malcolm MacDonald was sent to Dublin, but he was unable to get de Valera to promise to join the British war effort even in return for the ending of partition. Nevertheless members of the British cabinet considered compelling Northern Ireland to accept just such a bargain on 25 June 1940. They were so intent on securing Irish bases that Chamberlain suggested that Belfast should be told that 'the interests of Northern Ireland could not be allowed to stand against the vital interests of the British Empire.'[5]

The British decided to offer to accept 'the principle of a United Ireland' on condition that the Dublin government would 'enter the war on the side of the United Kingdom and her allies forthwith.' The offer was to be made as if Belfast would have no say in the matter, but the cabinet actually decided that if de Valera agreed, then Northern Ireland would be consulted.

In accordance with the plan, which MacDonald presented to de Valera next day, a commission consisting of representatives from Dublin and Belfast would be established to work out the constitutional and practical details of the proposed union. In addition, the British furnished a detailed list of weapons that they would be willing to supply once Ireland agreed to enter the war.

On meeting MacDonald to discuss these proposals on 27 June 1940, de Valera was accompanied by Aiken and Lemass.[6] The latter showed considerable interest in the offer. He suggested that the British should be satisfied if, without actually declaring war, Dublin simply invited them to defend Ireland and offered them bases for that purpose. In that way the onus of declaring war would be placed on the Germans.

Both de Valera and Aiken were obviously concerned by the line that Lemass was taking, as they frequently interrupted him. Aiken, who was convinced that Germany would win the war within six weeks,[7] was insistent that Ireland had a right to both unity and neutrality. De Valera also emphasised the same point. He noted, in addition, that the terms of the offer were too vague, because Belfast could sabotage the arrangement by making impossible demands on the commission drawing up the constitution. Nobody could have been unaware of the tremendous similarity beween the British offer and the avowed aims of the Irish Convention that Lloyd George had established and then ignored during World War I.

Even if London could give a firm guarantee of unity to de Valera, MacDonald predicted that offer would be rejected. The emissary reported that he was definitely of the opinion that 'the cabinet here will reject our plan.'

On 29 June Chamberlain explained in a letter to the Taoiseach that Britain would accept the approach suggested by Lemass which would not necessitate an Irish declaration of war, but he went on to note that the overall proposals were conditional on Belfast's acceptance. 'I cannot, of course, give a guarantee that Northern Ireland will assent,' the former Prime Minister wrote, 'but if the plan is accepted by Éire we should do our best to persuade Northern Ireland to accept it also in the interests of the security of the whole island.'[8]

That same day Lord Craigavon, the Northern Ireland Prime Minister, left little doubt about his attitude to the plan when he publicly complained that there was 'sinister evidence that something serious is afoot', with the result that he therefore wished to declare that he would 'be no party, directly or indirectly, to any change in the constitution conferred upon Northern Ireland, which assures us full partnership in the United Kingdom and British Empire.'[9]

De Valera informed Richard Mulcahy, one of the Fine Gael members of the Defence Conference, of the details of the British proposals on 2 July 1940. Although Mulcahy offered his party's support should the government decide to accept them, the Taoiseach explained that he was rejecting the proposals, which he characterised as so vague as not to actually constitute an offer.[10]

Privately Mulcahy did not think that even working together de Valera and Cosgrave would be able to carry the Dáil on the British terms. He estimated that only about half the members of Fianna Fáil would support the Taoiseach.[11] James Dillon, the deputy leader of Fine Gael and the only member of the Dáil to openly advocate abandoning neutrality during the war, came to essentially the same conclusion. He told Gray that neither the Dáil nor the country would tolerate an alliance with Britain at the time, because it seemed that the British were on the verge of defeat following the fall of France some days earlier.[12] 'We believed that if we were foolish enough to accept that invitation,' de Valera explained years later, 'we would have been cheated in the end.'[13] It should not therefore have been a surprise to anyone that the British proposals were turned down.

'The plan would involve our entry into the war,' de Valera wrote to Chamberlain. 'That is a course for which we could not accept responsibility. Our people would be quite unprepared for it, and Dáil Éireann would reject it.'[14]

The following November when Churchill sparked the press campaign for the ports, de Valera emphasised that while he was anxious for friendship with Britain, this was impossible while differences still existed. 'Unfortunately,' he explained to the Dáil on 7 November 1940, 'that outstanding matter, the matter of partition, which affects so deeply everyman and every woman of Irish blood throughout the world, was left unsettled, and it remained unsettled at the outset of this war.'

The Taoiseach was not content with simply stating his case in the Dáil, he also appealed directly for American help. In an open telegram to the president of AARIR, he asked 'all friends of Ireland to organise and put the Irish case, including partition, clearly before the American public'.[15] This was an indication to the London government that notwithstanding Britain's staunch support from the Roosevelt administration, Dublin was prepared to go over the heads of officials in Washington and appeal directly for American public support in order to embarrass Britain and thereby damage her much needed American aid, if she violated Irish neutrality. It was a strong reminder to the British leader that while Ireland did not have a well-equipped army, she had something more important — the emotional attachment of millions of Irish-Americans, who exerted a strong political influence in the United States, especially within the ruling Democratic Party.

During the war de Valera highlighted the partition issue by acting as if Northern Ireland was part of his own government's territory. He let it be known, for example, that he appreciated Germany's effective recognition of Irish sovereignty by not bombing the Six Counties.[16] When the Germans did make a heavy attack on Belfast a few months later, the Taoiseach instructed fire brigades from the Twenty-six Counties to proceed to the city and give whatever help possible, which was undoubtedly a violation of neutrality, but he made no apologies for helping the people of Belfast. 'They are all our people,' he declared, 'and their sorrows in the present instance are also our sorrows; and I want to say that any help we can give them in the present time we will give to them wholeheartedly, believing that were the circumstances reversed they would also give us their help wholeheartedly.'[17]

The following month when the British announced that they were thinking of introducing conscription in Northern Ireland, de Valera immediately objected. He tried at first discreetly to disabuse Churchill of the idea, and then he sought to enlist American and Canadian diplomatic pressure. At one point the Taoiseach agreed to an American suggestion that only the Roman Catholic community in the Six Counties should be exempted from compulsory military service, but he quickly reversed himself and demanded that conscription should not be applied to any people in the area.[18]

Before the war the Taoiseach had envisaged that the introduction of conscription would precipitate a crisis that would not only undermine his government but spark a revolution somewhat similar to what had happened during World War I. He was therefore genuinely concerned. 'Why at this critical time this new apple of discord should be thrown in, I cannot understand,' he wrote. 'If Mr Churchill is determined, as he seems to be, to go ahead with the proposal, the prospect is indeed as dark as it can be,' because conscription would almost inevitably 'lead to a new conflict between Ireland and Britain in which we shall all be involved. We are truly in a world gone mad.'[19]

The Taoiseach made a final appeal to Churchill not to allow the 'feeling of better understanding and mutual sympathy' which 'had grown up between our peoples in recent years' to be undermined by 'the imposition of conscription', as it would 'inevitably undo all the good that has been done and throw the two peoples back into the old unhappy relations.'[20] When there was no sign of the diplomatic efforts bearing fruit, de Valera went before the Dáil and openly denounced the proposed move. He was supported by the two principal opposition leaders. There could be little doubt that enforcing conscription in the Six Counties would have led to considerable unrest, which would almost certainly have had repercussions in the Twenty-six Counties. It was after all the conscription issue which had fatally damaged the Irish Parliamentary Party twenty-three years earlier. Most of Churchill's own colleagues appreciated the situation, and with the help of Sir Robert Menzies, the Prime Minister of Australia who was visiting Britain at the time, together with strong representations from both Washington and Ottawa, they prevailed upon the Prime Minister to abandon the scheme.

De Valera's success in staving off conscription in Northern Ireland, if anything, only hardened his attitude on the question of Irish sovereignty over the area. When he learned that American technicians were building a base on Lough Foyle some weeks later, for example, he told Gray that Irish authorities expected to be consulted if the United States ever decided to use the base, or any other facilities in Northern Ireland. The Taoiseach explained that while he recognised Britain's '*de facto* occupation of the Six Coun-

ties', he was not waiving Dublin's claim to sovereignty over
the area. Gray responded by indignantly suggesting that
the Irish Minister should be instructed to take up the question in Washington.[21]

Following further publicity concerning the American
technicians, de Valera instructed Brennan to seek an
explanation from the State Department, but that approach
was met with a blunt diplomatic snub. The State Department explained that the men were working in an area which
the United States considered British territory, with the
result that the inquiry should have been directed to the
British government.[22]

That was not the only American rebuff which de Valera
was to receive on the question of recognising sovereignty
over Northern Ireland. In January 1942 the Americans
ignored his warning to Gray and stationed troops in the Six
Counties without consulting Dublin.

The Taoiseach reacted by issuing a statement denouncing partition as 'one of the cruelist wrongs that can be
committed against a people.' Comparing Ireland's case
with the partitioning of Poland, he observed that the evils
that followed from it were no less 'than those which
Abraham Lincoln foresaw from the projected partition of
the United States, when he determined to prevent it, even
at the cost of fighting one of the bitterest civil wars in
history.' Then alluding to the American servicemen, de
Valera declared that 'no matter what troops occupy the Six
Counties, the Irish people's claim for the union of the
whole national territory and for supreme jurisdiction over
it will remain unabated.' He concluded that the 'maintenance of the partition of Ireland is as indefensible as the
aggressions against small nations elsewhere, which it is the
avowed purpose of Great Britain and the United States in
this war to bring to an end.'[23]

The American Minister in Dublin bitterly resented what
he considered a blatant attempt to put the United States
and Britain on the same moral plane as the fascist states. In
particular he was annoyed that de Valera should have
denounced the landing of Americans on what was supposedly Irish soil, when the Irish government had not

protested against the German bombings of Belfast several months earlier.

The incident made a lasting impression on Gray, who grew apprehensive about de Valera's disruptive potential — not just on the Irish scene, but also on the broader international stage. The American Minister was afraid, for instance, that the Irish leader might induce Irish-Americans to oppose whatever political settlement would be concluded in the post-war period just as after the First World War when he went to the United States and helped to turn Irish-Americans against the Versailles Treaty. As Gray saw the situation, there was no possibility that the Allies would force Belfast to accept Irish unity, especially after Northern Ireland had actively co-operated with the Allies, while Dublin had remained aloof during the war. Once the post-war peace conference rejected the Dublin government's claims, Gray feared that de Valera would go to the United States and actively compaign against the peace agreement in much the same way as he had opposed the Versailles Treaty in 1919.

Faced with the possibility that American isolationists would oppose the future settlement on ideological grounds and that they would be joined by many Republicans for purely partisan political reasons, the defection of the normally Democratic Irish-Americans could prove very damaging to the Roosevelt administration — especially as there was the obvious danger that other large Democratic ethnic groups, the German, Italian, and Polish-Americans, were likely to be dissatisfied with any probable settlement. Consequently all of the ingredients were prevalent for a repetition of the debacle surrounding the American rejection of the Versailles Treaty.

From Gray's own conversations in Dublin, he concluded that de Valera really did not want the majority in Northern Ireland to agree to the ending of partition, because if the eight hundred thousand Northern Irish Protestants were represented in an all-Ireland parliament, they would possess a balance of power and would hold an inordinate influence over Irish affairs. Thus the American Minister concluded that the only solution acceptable to de Valera would be a settlement whereby the Protestants in the Six Counties would be moved to Britain and replaced by a similar number of Roman Catholics of Irish extraction from Britain. This impression was strengthened when the Taoiseach told him on 3 June 1943 that Irish unity was not beyond the capability of good statesmanship, especially as 'exchanges of population were not impossible in these days.'[24]

Gray never considered the transfer of populations a practical proposition, which was hardly surprising for an American seeing that calling for the transfer of Northern Protestants, who could trace their roots in Ulster back to the early 1600s, would be like asking the great majority of Americans to leave the United States in order to give the area back to the Indians. Crediting the Irish leader with a formidable political acumen, he found in difficult to believe that de Valera thought an exchange of populations was feasible. Instead, he believed that the Taoiseach was simply exploiting the unity issue for domestic political purposes.

With the wartime privations under which Ireland was suffering likely to continue for sometime after the war in view of the probable reluctance of the Allies to make sacrifices for the Irish after the Dublin government's aloofness during the conflict, Gray thought that de Valera would not only attempt to excuse his wartime policy by contending that the wrongs of partition had compelled his government to remain neutral but that he would also try to create a rift between Britain and the United States in order to enlist American support for a campaign overtly designed to end partition but really intended only to strength his own political power and influence.

From as early as November 1942, therefore, Gray was advocating ways of preventing de Valera from poisoning Anglo-American relations. He thought, for instance, if the Taoiseach's protest over the arrival of American troops in Northern Ireland were 'suitably exploited in America', it would likely 'make it easier for the American government to maintain a friendly and co-operative policy toward Britain.'[25] One way of exploiting the situation was by formally requesting the Dublin government to join the Allied war effort so that the almost certain refusal could be given extensive publicity. Although he was able to explain the plan to Roosevelt and Churchill personally while visiting the United States during the summer of 1943, the State Department opposed the scheme on the grounds that de Valera might comply with the request and abandon neutrality, thus leaving the Allies with the moral obligation of diverting men and material to defend Irish towns and cities. The American chiefs of staff had already warned that Ireland's adherence to the Allied cause would likely be a liability because Irish ports and bases were of no value as long as the Germans controlled the French coast. Consequently it was decided in Washington that Roosevelt should only ask the Taoiseach to promise to make Irish bases available if those should be needed at a later date, but the British vetoed that proposal, apparently because they were afraid that de Valera might comply and would then be in an even stronger position to make trouble over partition after the war.[26]

Gray next suggested that Roosevelt should simply ask for the expulsion of German and Japanese representatives from Ireland, ostensibly on the grounds that they were an espionage threat to the planned Allied invasion of Europe. The proposal was motivated by political, rather than military considerations. Gray was mainly interested in getting de Valera's refusal on record. 'I think,' he wrote to one State Department official, 'it would be very unfortunate to let this situation slip away without at least reaping the political benefit which we both believe would be obtained by a refusal on the part of the Irish Government to comply with such a request.'[27] In another letter some weeks later he wrote that 'the only choice' was whether American authorities would face up to the devisive threat posed by the partition question 'while the war continues, while Anglo-American solidarity is strong, while American obligation to Northern Ireland for facilities is remembered, or to wait upon a time and circumstance favourable to Mr de Valera.'[28]

What the American Minister wanted was to be able to

contrast Anglo-American co-operation — especially the role that Northern Ireland played in that co-operation — with de Valera's refusal to help the United States. He therefore believed that getting the Taoiseach to refuse to expel Axis representatives from Ireland would be a particularly effective way of highlighting the whole issue, because it would involve the emotive issue of 'a threat to the lives of American soldiers', which, Gray wrote, would 'unfailingly excite American resentment'.[29]

As we have seen in the preceeding chapter, the scheme worked. The American press was bitterly critical of the Irish refusal to expel the Axis representatives, and de Valera was widely depicted as a Nazi sympathiser, but the Taoseach turned his own stand to political advantage at home by calling an election in which Fianna Fáil gained seventeen seats to give the party a comfortable majority in the Dáil. As a result Irish writers have tended to view de Valera as the victor in his confrontations with the American Minister, but this has not been an accurate picture because the latter had been trying to discredit de Valera in American eyes and was not upset by the Irish election results. He realised that there were difficult times ahead for the Fianna Fáil government, which would be held responsible for the country's post-war privations, so he welcomed de Valera's victory. 'He is now in for five more years and if his mistakes are what we think they are, he will have to liquidate them. There was a danger that he would duck responsibility for a while and let the opposition pay the bills and clean the slate and then come back when they bungled.'[30]

After the war de Valera had to bide his time before launching his long postponed anti-partition campaign. For one thing his reputation had been seriously tarnished as a result of Gray's exploits, and time would be needed for emotions to cool down. He therefore exerted his energies in discreetly encouraging anti-partition groups that were being independently formed in Northern Ireland, Britain and the United States.

Some people suggested that membership of the United Nations Organisation would further the country's aim of complete national independence, but he did not share their optimism. He nevertheless advocated joining the organisation as the most effective means available of defending the advances already made.[31] In so doing, he demonstrated that he was not the selfish isolationist so often depicted by Allied propagandists.

The Taoiseach openly called, for example, for 'something like a world confederation'. In advocating that the country apply for membership of the United Nations he candidly warned the Dáil that the Irish people should be prepared to uphold the obligations under the Charter even if it meant becoming involved in a military conflict. 'The difference between a war such as may arise under the obligations of the Charter and other wars is,' he explained, 'that that type of war would be a war of enforcement, enforcement of obligations and also enforcement of rights. If there is ever to be a rule of law, nations must make up their minds that they will take part in such enforcement, because, if there is not enforcement, then, of course, the duties and rights that are guaranteed will be thrown aside.' He added that he felt it would have been the country's duty to participate in military measures against Italy during the Ethiopian conflict, if the League had determined on such action. Consequently he wanted it clearly understood before joining the United Nations that if the country was called upon to fight in order to uphold the Charter's obligations, 'our people will be fortified by the knowledge that it is their duty to fulfil them and that they will not be taken by surprise in having to deal with a situation of that sort.'[32]

When the Dublin government subsequently applied for membership of the United Nations, however, the application was vetoed by the Soviet Union on the supposed grounds that Ireland had not only failed to help the Allies during the war, but had maintained cordial relations with the enemy yet refused to open diplomatic relations with th Soviet Union. 'Her behaviour,' Foreign Minister Andre Gromyko explained, 'is hardly calculated to help her to admission to the United Nations.'[33] But it was not long before de Valera welcomed the fact that Ireland was denied membership at the time, because of course it relieved the country of any responsibility for becoming involved in the Korean War.

Meanwhile de Valera gradually revived his efforts to secure Irish unity, but his government was being faced with serious economic difficulties as many commodities continued to be in short supply after the war. Although he called for an increase in wheat production, the summer of 1946 was one of the wettest on record, with the result that the harvest yield was so bad that bread rationing had to be reintroduced. Then conditions were complicated by one of the century's harshest winters and a serious energy crisis brought about by a drastic reduction in coal exports from Britain. Industry was seriously disrupted and transportation almost paralysed. Seán Lemass, the Minister for Supplies, declared on 3 January 1947 that the country was confronted with a situation 'more difficult than at any stage of the war.' But de Valera still found time to stress the partition issue in his St Patrick's Day address to the United States. He asked listeners for their support in his efforts to achieve Irish unity. 'The Irishmen who help are securing the foundations for a splendid future of our nation,' he said. 'It is for that reason that I can confidently ask all you who are listening to me to lend your support.'[34]

James Dillon, who was still in the political wilderness as a result of being forced to resign from Fine Gael for openly advocating that the country abandon neutrality during the war, denounced de Valera's obvious attempts to interfere in American affairs by trying to get Irish-Americans to influence their country's foreign policy. Dillon contended that Irish policy was really aimed at driving a wedge between the United States and Britain at a crucial time when Anglo-American solidarity was vital to check the menacing threat to democracy being posed by the Soviet Union. Dillon advocated that instead of exploiting the situation with divisive activities, the Taoiseach should help in the protection of the western democracies by allowing the United States to use Irish bases. Otherwise, he warned, there was a danger that the Soviet politbureau would use Ireland 'to achieve the diabolical ends which Moscow has in mind.'[35]

On 24 June 1947 de Valera told the Dáil he still believed that British leaders were privately in favour of Irish unity, and he suggested it would be helpful if they would give public expression to their private feelings in the matter. 'I think that it would make for a solution of this problem,' he said, 'if at the present time the British Government would make a simple declaration to the effect that they were desirous of seeing partition brought to an end, that they would do anything that they could do to help bring it to an end, and that if agreement were reached here in Ireland, there would be no hesitation on their part in giving effect to the agreement.' Until such a declaration was forthcoming, the Taoiseach said that Dublin had to face the reality that it could 'only deal with this problem on the basis that there are three parties, the concurrence of whose wills will have to be brought about before partition can be ended.' Adding that the only two ways of bringing about unity would be by force or by persuasion, he said that he had long ago ruled out the use of force, because even if force were successful, it would leave the state 'in an unstable position'. Consequently the only course open was to follow a policy of persuasion, in which he believed that public opinion in the United States and Britain could play an important role.[36]

A couple of days later Gray, who was retiring as United States Minister the following week, warned that the continued effort to put political pressure on Washington would 'inevitably result in a sense of grievance and irritation' in America. As international tension was mounting in the face of the Soviet menace, he suggested that the Taoiseach should co-operate with Anglo-American efforts to make the British Isles a bridgehead for the defence of the west. But de Valera refused to consider the idea.

'We are free,' he said interrupting with some vehemence, 'but only in part. We can take no part in the kind of thing you suggest while this wrong to our six northern counties continues.'

'What do you wish us to do about it?' Gray asked impatiently; 'do you want us to send troops into the Six Counties to conquer them and hand them over to you?'

'Of course not,' replied the Taoiseach.

'The only other course is in your own hands,' Gray observed; 'that is, to make conditions so desirable in Éire that the North will wish to join you.'

'But,' de Valera persisted, 'if we cannot ask you to coerce the Six Counties why should the *Protestant* majority coerce the nationalist minorities in two of them?'

'Suppose, for the sake of argument,' replied Gray, 'we were able to arrange the handing over to you of the two counties of which you speak, would you not still have partition as to the remaining four? Would not the crime against your sovereignty of which you complain still subsist?'[37]

According to the American Minister, de Valera did not answer.

Although the Taoiseach had admitted that persuasion was the only course open to his government on the partition issue, he still refused to show any inclination to compromise on the stands that his government had taken on the questions of republicanism, or the efforts to revive Irish as the spoken language of the people. 'I do not see why,' he said, 'the people in this part of Ireland should sacrifice ideals which they hold dear — completely sacrifice those ideals in order to meet the views of people whose position fundamentally is not as just or as right as our position is.' He added that the existing association with the British Commonwealth was 'the farthest we could go to meet their views in the North.'[38]

Just what that association was at the time caused a good deal of confusion. Nobody seemed quite sure whether the government considered the country a member of the Commonwealth or not, and de Valera did little to clarify the situation for a long time. When pressed on the issue on one occasion in July 1945, for example, he simply responded that 'in all political systems there are relationships which it is wiser to leave undefined.'[39] What he did say sometime later was that 'if being in the Commonwealth implied in any way allegiance or acceptance of the British King as King here, we are not in the Commonwealth.'[40]

Notwithstanding the country's association with the Commonwealth, the Taoiseach held that the country was really an independent republic. 'Twenty-six of our counties are a republic,' he told a gathering in Dublin on 26 October 1947, and if the Irish nation continued to give Fianna Fáil support, the party would have 'a better chance of securing the whole of Ireland as a republic than any other party.' He was undoubtedly alluding to Clann na Poblachta, a party recently formed under the leadership of the eminent lawyer, Seán MacBride, who was a former chief of staff of the IRA and a son of one of the executed leaders of 1916. The new party had been making serious inroads into Fianna Fáil's traditional support, especially among republican elements. So in an obvious effort to deny MacBride and his colleagues the time necessary to organise themselves properly, the Taoiseach called a general election for February 1948.

During the election campaign he declared that he was ready to take up his anti-partition efforts where they had been interrupted by the Second World War. He even announced, for example, that after the election he would go to the United States to drum up American support and that he would also appeal to other countries for help. While the timing of those announcements was undoubtedly influenced by campaign tactics to outmanoeuvre Clann na Poblachta, there could be no doubt that his plans had indeed been interrupted by the war. Moreover, in recent months he had been discreetly encouraging the formation of organisations like the American League for an Undivided Ireland in the United States and the Anti-Partition League in Britain to organise public support in favour of Irish unity in their respective countries.

'I promise,' de Valera declared at an election rally in Sligo, 'that the pressure of public opinion of the Irish race, not in Ireland only, but throughout the world, will be concentrated on this question.' He made it clear that he intended to enlist the support of 'public opinion not only of those who have Irish blood in their veins, but of their fellow citizens — men and women — of other races, who also believe in justice and know that only on the basis of justice can peace between neighbouring peoples be secured.'[41]

It would have been futile to launch such a campaign for overseas support during the war, especially in the United

States, where interest in ethnic affairs had virtually ceased following the country's entry into the war in 1941. Being primarily Americans, the Irish-Americans obviously felt that ethnic considerations should be put aside so that they could devote their full attention to the prosecution of the war. As a result Irish considerations faded into insignificance, as was evidenced by the disbanding of the American Friends of Irish Neutrality within a few days of the Pearl Harbour attack. But by late 1947 there were signs of a resurgence of American interest in ethnic affairs with the staging of Ireland's premier sporting event, the All-Ireland Gaelic Football Final in New York, and the convening in the same city some weeks later of an Irish Race Convention, which attracted some six hundred delegates from the forty-eight states. The Convention decided to establish the American League for an Undivided Ireland to organise American opinion against partition.

While the resurgence of ethnic activities was noticeable against the backdrop of the wartime inactivity, its importance was exaggerated in Irish newspapers, especially the *IrishPress,* which tended to give the impression that there was a great mass of American opinion deeply interested in Irish affairs and prepared to campaign vociferously for the ending of partition, whereas in fact, the Irish Race Convention was virtually ignored by the American newspapers, which were primarily interested in the news of the Truman administration's efforts to get congress to authorise the Marshall Plan to ward off threatening disaster in Europe.

From the Irish standpoint the resurgence of American interest in ethnic affairs was probably most significant in that it gave rise to hopes that an international campaign could be successfully waged against partition, which in turn might reasonably have been expected to enhance de Valera's electoral appeal, seeing that he was the logical person to exploit the situation as he had by far the greatest international standing of any Irish politician. Yet to what extent such considerations actually influenced the Irish electorate must remain a matter of conjecture, because while de Valera's party lost its majority in the Dáil and he was himself replaced as Taoiseach by John A. Costello at the head of a coalition government, Fianna Fáil was still easily the largest party in the Dáil, and Clann na Poblachta fared comparatively badly at the polls by winning only ten seats.

Despite the election set-back, de Valera still went ahead with his planned visit to the United States. The trip, which lasted for four weeks, took in various American cities, including Washington, D.C., where he had a private meeting with President Truman. The Fianna Fáil leader told the press afterwards that the President and himself had 'just had a friendly chat' and 'did not discuss anything serious.'[42] Other major stops on his itinerary included New York City, San Francisco, Los Angeles, Chicago, Detroit, Philadelphia, Providence, and Boston. He explained that his visit was to thank Americans for their past assistance in the struggle for Irish independence and to request further help. 'I have come to thank you now,' he told a radio audience in Chicago, 'and I have also come to ask for it again in the struggle for the freedom of Ireland.'[43]

De Valera's attitude towards the Irish question in relation to the overall international picture was strikingly similar to the views he expressed almost three decades earlier. Just as he had been critical of the League of Nations for excluding Ireland in 1919, he was now critical that the country was being denied membership of the United Nations Organisation by the veto of the Soviet Union. He therefore predicted that the new organisation was not likely to be any more effective than its predecessor.

'I am not optimistic about avoiding war,' he told a radio audience in Los Angeles. 'I had more hope for the success of the League of Nations than of the United Nations Organisation. As the position stands I see the inevitable drift to war unless a miracle changes the nations' wills.'[44]

He left no doubt about the role that he thought that Ireland should play in any coming conflict. Ireland should remain neutral, he said, although the prime reason that he put forward to justify that policy was somewhat confused. At a press conference shortly after his arrival in New York, for example, he said that he favoured neutrality because Ireland was too small to be effective and would therefore only be hurt in another major war. 'It is a matter of life or death for a small nation to take such a decision,' he explained. 'Where a big power takes a decision to enter a war, it has the force necessary to fight for what it wants, and a small nation has not. When the peace came the big power could get what it fought for; a small nation might not have the power to do so.'[45]

The Fianna Fáil leader indicated later, however, that the principal reason for pursuing neutrality would be because Dublin could not co-operate with Britain while the latter continued to act in what he considered an unjust fashion towards Ireland by maintaining partition. 'Nations cannot co-operate with nations if such injustices are permitted,' he declared. 'The only basis of co-operation must be that of justice. At present anything else is stupid.'[46]

The lack of such basic justice, he argued, was the real reason for Irish nationalists refusing to become involved in the two World Wars. 'We refused to fight in World War I for what they called the freedom of small nations, because our territory was occupied by Britain and we resented injustice,' he explained. 'We could not have been expected to fight in World War II unless we were attacked. Our territory was still occupied by Britain, and the injustice continued.'[47] In New York he actually implied that Ireland would like to stand with the democracies in the coming conflict against the Soviet Union, whose actions he believed were making war inevitable.

'We want to play our part in the world, in trying to bring about a better world,' de Valera stated, but he added that democracy should be allowed 'to work in Ireland as it works elsewhere.'[48]

In trying to put partition into an American perspective, the former Irish leader grossly oversimplified by equating the political differences between the two segments of Ireland with the differences between the two largest political parties in the United States. 'Ireland is cut in two without the consent of the Irish,' he said. 'You would reduce democracy to an absurdity if you cut off a block of states voting by majority Republican or Democrat. People who preach democracy for other nations have reduced it to an absurdity in Ireland.'[49]

Not content with simply implying criticism of Britain's undemocratic action, de Valera openly denounced the role of the British in Northern Ireland. 'They tell you that what they call Ulster must not be coerced,' he said in Boston. 'Answer them that it is being coerced, that the majority of the people of four of the cut-off counties and the great minority in the rest are being held in territory garrisoned by British arms against their own wishes to unite with the rest of Ireland.'[50]

'If what is happening in partitioned Ireland today were being done in Eastern Europe by Russia,' he added, 'the people on whom it was being done would be entitled to ask [for] assistance, and many who talk of democracy now would cry out against the injustice.' He actually went so far as to contend that Britain was acting more undemocratically than the Soviet Union, because the British were partitioning Ireland in the name of democracy, while he said that the Russians just acted blatantly without the pretence of any worthy motive.

'If I were Stalin, and wanted what Stalin wanted,' the Fianna Fáil leader told the National Press Club in Washington, D.C., 'I would imitate Britain and get away with it as Britain is getting away with it. It would be easy to pick an area somewhere in Europe with a Communist majority and, on pretence of safeguarding a minority, to cut off that area, and make it appear as if it were being governed by a majority.'[51]

According to de Valera the ending of partition would be a step towards world peace. 'Let those asking for world peace realise that in undoing partition they are going far to help world peace,' he said. 'If any nation imposes its will on another, it will be resented and will inevitably lead to war. If we neglect to secure justice for any nation, even the smallest, we are on the road to war.'[52]

In seeking justice for Ireland, he tried to portray himself as being prepared to lean over backwards to satisfy the Northern majority. He said that he would allow Northern Ireland to keep Stormont with its existing powers although it was not entitled to them. If, however, the Northern majority was not willing to accept such a compromise, then he felt that they should not be allowed to impede union and should therefore be bought off and obviously transferred elsewhere. 'We would say to them that we would prefer that you stay,' he explained, 'but if you prefer an outside power we cannot have our unity threatened by your loyalty. If you don't want to be Irish, we are prepared to let you go and compensate you. It will pay us because ill-will between the two countries would be a danger to both. We do not want to be kept in disunion because of a small minority.'[53]

Before concluding his American tour, de Valera announced his intention of visiting Australia and New Zealand. He then returned to Dublin for a large anti-partition rally in College Green, Dublin, before setting out for Australia, ostensibly to honour Daniel Mannix, the Irish-born Roman Catholic Archbishop of Melbourne who was celebrating the golden jubilee of his ordination to the priesthood.

While in Australia, where he remained for six weeks, de Valera quickly sought to explain why Ireland had failed to come to Britain's aid, as Australia had, during the recent war. He laid the blame on Britain for partitioning Ireland and thus creating a situation which left the Dublin government with no alterative but to remain neutral. 'Had part of our soil and people not been kept from us by force,' he told a Melbourne gathering shortly after his arrival, 'our conduct in 1939 might — I repeat might — have been different, but while that cruel injustice persisted there could not be any question of the Irish participating in the war.'[54]

Throughout his stay he repeatedly denounced partition and Britain's reponsibility for it. He told an Adelaide crowd that 'only a bandit' could act in such an unjust manner.[55]

Following a four-day stay in New Zealand de Valera started his return journey, with brief stops in Ceylon, Burma, and India, where he met with Prime Minister Pandit Nehru and the latter's daughter, Indira Ghandi. Next he stopped in Rome, where he told a press conference that if the Northern Irish element was 'so attached to Britain, and wanted to opt for Britain, we will let them go to Britain.'[56]

Afterwards he had a meeting with the Italian Premier, Alcide de Gasperi, and then visited the Vatican for an audience with Pope Pius XII and acting Secretary of State, Monsignor Giovani Montini (later Pope Paul VI).

De Valera arrived back in Dublin just in time for the Fianna Fáil Árd Fheis, at which he received a tumultuous welcome on 22 June 1948. He told the convention that he had plans for a world wide effort against partition and had already prepared the ground for campaigns in the United States, Australia and New Zealand, and hoped that similar efforts could also be organised in Canada, South Africa and India. 'We have a splendid case,' he said. 'Partition is on a rotten foundation and it will totter and end. All we want to do is make up our mind to make the proper assault.'

Since being forced into opposition, the Fianna Fáil leader's attitude towards partition had been showing distinct signs of hardening because, as one authority concluded, de Valera threw discretion to the winds.'[57] Speaking in the Dáil in July 1948, for instance, he criticised the Minister for External Affairs, Seán MacBride, for not challenging a new British nationality act on the grounds 'that our citizens in the Six Counties, who are natural-born Irish citizens owing allegiance to this country and to no other,' were being 'bound and dealt with exactly as if they were citizens of Britain.'[58]

'We cannot have in this country people whose first allegiance is not to our nation,' the Fianna Fáil leader added, 'and we should make it clear, that if there are such people, that we do not regard as our citizens, and we should know where we stand in respect of them. What they are, to which country they are loyal will only appear in times of crisis; we are in a time of crisis.'

Observing the recent hardening in de Valera's attitude, some people suggested that it was simply because he had been relieved of the responsibility of office and could speak out with blatant disregard for the consequences of Britain's reaction. They questioned why he had only recently begun to speak out in such a manner.

'The reason was,' de Valera explained, 'that we have

been doing things in regular order.'[59] He believed that it would only be possible to end partition once the issue had been isolated, and all other outstanding issues had been settled. He therefore appealed to his audience to call on their relatives abroad to speak out and use their influence to exert pressure for the ending of partition.

'The people of the six partitioned counties are our brothers,' he said the following week. 'They want to be with us and we swear before Heaven that we shall never give up until they are with us.' If that was not an emotive exaggeration, it was no worse than his reference to the economic set-up in which he declared that the standard of living in the Twenty-six Counties was not only higher than that in Northern Ireland but that 'there is probably not in the whole world at the present a country in which there is such a decent standard of living as there is in this part of Ireland.'[60]

The coalition government tried to outflank de Valera by repealing the External Relations Act of 1936 and formally declaring the Twenty-six Counties, the Republic of Ireland, thereby officially withdrawing from the Commonwealth and thus ending the confusion over Irish membership. In addition, the coalition took the initiative for an anti-partition campaign and also carried the Fianna Fáil government's policy of neutrality a step further by refusing an invitation to join the North Atlantic Treaty Organisation (NATO). Although the declaration of the Republic of Ireland was psychologically a momentous occasion, it was not very important from the practical standpoint, as de Valera had long ago fulfilled the promise he had made in April 1933 to dismantle the 1921 Treaty to such an extent that the declaration of a republic would only be a mere formality. He did not therefore raise any objections to the repeal of the External Relations Act. In fact, he had actually taken some steps for its repeal before leaving office himself.

Before the new legislation became law the government invited de Valera to an all-party conference at the Mansion House, Dublin, on 27 January 1949, with a view to organising a campaign to end partition. There, Costello announced that Ireland was ready to hit 'Britain in her pride, prestige and pocket.' The fanfare with which the anti-partition drive was launched was probably the strongest show of solidarity between the Irish political parties since the Mansion House Conference of 1918 had been convoked to oppose British efforts to introduce conscription in Ireland during the First World War.

De Valera welcomed the initiative. In fact, he contended that the actions of the Costello government were 'strictly in accordance with the plan and the programme announced by Fianna Fáil at its inaugural meeting nearly twenty-three years ago. We then set before us the securing of full independence for this part of Ireland as the first step on which we would concentrate, so that this being achieved, the problem of partition might be isolated for the combined and converging attack of all who loved Ireland or were concerned with the broad right of a nation to be free.'[61]

The Anti-Partition League began holding rallies in various English cities, and de Valera attended several of those in Birmingham, Sheffield, Newcastle and London. On 13 February 1949 he told a meeting in Newcastle that the counties where the nationalists were in a majority should be handed over to the Dublin government, but he did not pretend that he would be satisfied with such a settlement. It would obviously be only a step towards his ultimate goal.

'We demand that these counties where there is an overwhelming majority* against partition should be given back to us in all fairness and justice,' he said. 'But that would not solve the partition problem, because our ancient homeland would be severed and mutilated.'

When asked at a press conference in Newcastle that day what could be done about northern unionists who did not want Irish unity, the Fianna Fáil leader had a succinct answer. If they wanted to be Irish, he said, all they would have to do was accept democratic rule; but if they wanted to be British, then the only place they could get full satisfaction for their sentiments would be in Britain. In other words, the unionists should be transferred to Britain.

* In a general election the previous week, anti-partition candidates had a majority of 52.86 per cent in County Fermanagh, and 52.5 per cent in County Tyrone.

While de Valera made no pretence that the transfer of nationalist areas would be completely satisfactory, he was apparently deviating from government policy in even calling for the transfer of those areas. On visiting London for talks with the British a fortnight later, for example, MacBride stated that the Dublin government could not favour the simple return of Fermanagh and Tyrone, or other areas with anti-partition majorities. He explained that he was relying on the principle that Ireland was a single unit.[62] No doubt MacBride was afraid that if the nationalist areas were transferred from the Six Counties, then the nationalist minority in what would remain of Northern Ireland would be too small to pose a really significant force for Irish unity and the prospects for complete national independence might be irreparably damaged.

At the time the prospects of enlisting British support were growing dimmer. Just as the campaign against partition initiated in the autumn of 1938 had led to a hardening in the attitude of British officials, Irish agitation in 1949 had a similar effect. Instead of weakening Westminster's resolve to support the northern unionists, it greatly enhanced it. When there were rumours, following the declaration of the republic, that the British planned to declare formally that partition could only be ended with the consent of the majority in Northern Ireland, de Valera immediately denounced the suggestion.

'We in Ireland,' he declared, 'will definitely regard as a hostile act any declaration that we have to convert a minority in the Six Counties — a minority so arranged that it has a perpetual majority in government.'[63]

The British ignored de Valera's warning and introduced their own legislation clarifying their relationship with the Twenty-six Counties and stipulating that 'in no event will Northern Ireland or any part thereof cease to be part of His Majesty's dominions and of the United Kingdom without the consent of the Parliament of Northern Ireland.' That legislation was easily passed by a vote of 312 to only 12 in the House of Commons.

Meanwhile as the Costello government continued to refuse to enter NATO, de Valera supported the policy. He also opposed Irish membership in a proposed European federation when the whole idea was discussed at the Assembly of the Council of Europe in Strasbourg in August 1949. He pointed out that it would be very difficult to persuade the Irish people to enter such a federation at the time. It was after all a relatively short time since Ireland had been engaged in a struggle to break out of a union with Britain, and the Irish people would be naturally very sceptical about sacrificing their new found independence by entering an even larger union.[64]

'It must be obvious,' de Valera said, 'that it would be extremely difficult now to induce our people to reverse suddenly the whole current of their thought and history, and voluntarily to give up, or seriously endanger, that identity towards the preservation of which such glorious devotion has been shown and such sacrifices endured.' He explained that the whole situation was being complicated by partition. "I am sure you can understand with a cynical smile an Irish citizen would regard you if you spoke to him about uniting into a huge state the several states of Europe with their diverse national traditions so long as he contemplates his own country kept divided against his will.'

With each country likely to have its own special difficulties, de Valera explained that it was because of Ireland's own peculiar difficulties that he felt that she could not enter a federated Europe at that time, but he made it clear that he was not personally opposed to the idea of continental unity. 'If the nations here on the mainland of the continent consider that they cannot wait for us,' he said, 'perhaps they should consider going on without us by an agreement for a close union among themselves. It is from no desire to interfere with or delay them that some of us here have spoken against the attempt at immediate federation. It is simply because we know the task that would confront us in persuading our people to proceed by that road.'

According to one authority, de Valera was on the crest of an anti-partition wave while the coalition government was in the trough.[65] The government seemed to be pursuing essentially his policy — contending that Irish involvement in NATO or a European federation was out of the question while partition continued. Costello himself even followed his predecessor's example by appealing directly for American support for Irish unity in a St Patrick's Day address to the United States in 1950.

The efforts to involve American authorities did meet with a little success, but the whole partition issue was a bit of a political football, being kicked about by politicians playing to their own radical Irish-American constituents by proposing resolutions and introducing motions that had no real hope of passage in Congress.

Contending that the 'ficticious border between the North and the South of Ireland constitutes a threat to the peace and security of the world,' Representative T. J. Lane of Massachusetts introduced a bill calling for a ten-man commission to secure Irish unity in 1948.[66] The following year Representative John E. Fogarty of Rhode Island tried to have Britain excluded from Marshall Aid while partition lasted, and the year after that Senator Herbert Lehman of New York introduced a resolution calling for an end to partition. The following month Representative Mike Mansfield of Montana convened his sub-committee of the House Foreign Affairs Committee to hold hearings on the Irish question, and he subsequently co-sponsored a bill with Representative Jacob Javits of New York, calling for the United Nations to supervise a plebiscite in Ireland on the unity issue, but nothing ever came of any of those efforts.

However, there was what looked initially like a sensational breakthrough in late March 1950 when Fogarty managed to secure the approval of the House of Representatives for an amendment excluding some $687 millions in aid to Britain from an appropriations bill authorising the continuation of Marshall Aid. At the time he contended that the United States would, in effect, be subsidising partition with that money, because Britain was spending $150 millions annually in supporting the Stormont administration.[67]

As almost two thirds of the members of the House of Representatives were missing when the vote was taken, observers had no doubt that the Fogarty amendment would be eliminated before the bill finally became law, but this did not prevent some people from taking a very poor view of the political manoeuvring. In view of the overall international situation, the *New York Times* noted that the action had been irresponsible and would lead to 'real rejoicing' only in Moscow.[68] As expected, Congress did subsequently reinstate the aid to Britain before the bill was finalised.

The Costello government sought to use American concern over the international situation to its own advantage on the partition issue. MacBride, who was in the United States for St Patrick's Day, 1951, stressed during his visit that Ireland was anxious to assist the democracies in thwarting the threat posed by communism, but could not help as long as partition lasted. He told the National Press Club in Washington on 14 March 1951 that while the Irish government's concern over partition 'may seem exaggerated to the rest of the world', it was the cause of such emotional fervour among the Irish that no Dublin government could attempt to enter a military alliance with Britain 'without being driven from office'. He summarised the Irish position as being basically the same as that adopted by the de Valera government during the war. Ireland was anxious to play a full role in international affairs, he said, but she was being kept out of the United Nations Organisation by the Soviet Union and could not enter NATO because of the opposition of the Irish people towards any alliance involving Britain — the perpetrator of partition.

'The position then, in short,' MacBride said, 'is that Ireland is willing and anxious to play her full part in international affairs. That she is already making a contribution, but is prevented from doing her full share by two outside powers — Russia and Britain.'[69]

A few days later de Valera adopted basically the same stance in London. 'It is foolish to talk about good relations between Ireland and Britain,' he said, 'as long as the evil of partition exists.'[70] He had already declared that 'a divided Ireland would have no option but to remain neutral in a third world war.'[71]

When asked if he would agree to participate in such a war

if partition were ended, he adopted the same attitude as he had when Malcolm MacDonald made what was supposed to be such an offer in 1940. 'If you attempt to condition freedom,' de Valera said, 'you have not got it.'[72]

The only condition he was prepared to concede was the same one that he had been offering since 1921, that Dublin would permit Stormont to retain its existing powers, provided that those powers were applied impartially and the powers vested in Westminster were transferred to an all-Ireland parliament. He stressed, however, that there could be no question of the majority in the Six Counties remaining British. 'If they want to be Irish we will receive them with a heart and a half,' the Fianna Fáil leader said. 'But they must choose either to be Irish or British. They can't be both.'[73]

Within a few weeks the Costello government fell due to an internal squabble over domestic policy, after the Roman Catholic Archbishop of Dublin had demanded that some provisions of a health bill be amended on the grounds that the bill was too socialistic — which in the rather myopic view of the archbishop was apparently a move towards atheistic communism. When Noel Browne, the Minister of Health, refused to amend the bill, he was forced to resign, which gave rise to a political crisis that brought down the government. The whole affair seemed to confirm what Seán Ó Faoláin had described as the 'pervasive clerical control' of Irish life, which so frightened the majority in Northern Ireland.

The partition issue really played no part in the ensuing general election, which saw the return of de Valera to power at the head of a minority government on 13 June 1951. Once back in office he again began playing down the partition question. In July, for example, he opposed and thus virtually ensured the defeat of a proposal that would have allowed representatives elected in Northern Ireland to sit in the Dublin parliament.

At the time the new Taoiseach admitted that he could think of no policy which had any prospects of success 'within a reasonable time'. He again ruled out the use of military action to force 'the people of the North to come in', and he added that he did not believe there was any likelihood of being able 'to cajole them either'. He just advocated that the country should be prepared to make the best of any circumstances. 'I could not have told here at any time, for example, that the ports were going to come back, but I did have at the back of my mind that any situation which arose that would enable us to get those ports back should be availed of by us to do so,' he explained to the Dáil. 'Circumstances may come our way again — we cannot create them, we can only avail of them — which we may be able to utilise towards ending partition.' As things stood, he added, 'about one-third of the people in that area are our supporters and want to have the unity of the country. What you really have to win over is, therefore, the difference between one-third and one half, that is, one-sixth. He still hoped that the effort to enlist international support would bear some fruit.[74]

Within a matter of weeks there were some hopeful signs on the American scene when a resolution proposed by Congressman Fogarty was approved by the House Foreign Affairs Committee, expressing the sense of the house that the 'Republic of Ireland should embrace the entire territory of Ireland unless the clear majority of all the people of Ireland in a free plebiscite determine and declare to the contrary.'[75] In explaining its actions, the committee announced that 'an integrated and solidified Ireland could serve as a stronger bastion of collective security in the North Atlantic area at a time when the mutual security of the United States and our allies is so important.'[76]

De Valera warmly welcomed the actions of the Foreign Affairs Committee as 'a signal service not only to Ireland but to the advocates of democratic rights and duties everywhere.'[77] However, it soon became apparent that the House of Representatives as a whole did not share the committee's views, because it refused to act on the resolution the following month by a vote of 206 to 139.

Thereafter Congressional efforts to involve the United States in the Irish question met with little enthusiasm, or support. Efforts, however, to get candidates to take a stand on the partition issues did meet with some limited success in 1952 when the Republican Vice-Presidential nominee, Richard M. Nixon — a man not particularly well-known for his veracity either then or later — held out the possibility that if elected the Republicans would put pressure on Britain to end partition.

'One thing that occurs to me,' Nixon said during the 1952 campaign, 'is the possibility of putting pressure on the British when it comes to handling our American money. Then it would be made clear we do not favour their policy in relation to Ireland. It can be said there is a better chance of the Republican administration doing something about partition than the Democrats.' He added that the United States could exercise considerable moral pressure on Britain and he would endeavour to do so.[78]

Dwight D. Eisenhower, the Republican presidential nominee steered clear of the issue, but then he could not be expected to be very sympathetic with the Dublin government's views as he had already gone on record as lauding the fact that Northern Ireland's separation from the rest of the island had allowed her to co-operate with the Allies during the war. 'Without Northern Ireland I do not see how the American Forces could have been concentrated to begin the invasion of Europe,' Eisenhower told a Belfast gathering in 1945. 'If Ulster had not been a definite, co-operative part of the British Empire and had not been available for our use, I do not see how the build-up could have been carried out in England.'[79] In view of the delicate Cold War balance of power that existed throughout Eisenhower's years as President of the United States, it should not have been surprising that he never showed any interest in exerting pressure on either Britain or Northern Ireland to end partition.

But then de Valera himself continued to play down the partition issue during those years. Upon his return to power he had given the portfolio of External Affairs to Frank Aiken, and neither of them tried to revive the anti-partition campaign. In fact, de Valera actually criticised the campaign that had been conducted by the coalition government. If his predecessors had been serious about hitting Britain in her pride, prestige and pocket, he told a meeting in Drogheda on 28 February 1954, they would have expelled the British ambassador and would have severed all trade with Britain. Of course he did not advocate such a policy himself. He simply contended that a more moderate approach was needed. 'There is one policy which we can pursue,' he said, 'a policy of trying to establish decent relations between the people of Britain and the Six Counties and ourselves.'

De Valera actually had the startling audacity to contend that partition should not be made a political issue. 'I don't want to make partition a political issue,' he said, 'because I do not believe there is any one of the parties who have got the solution for it.' It was noteworthy when he visited Britain for St Patrick's Day a couple of weeks later, he stressed the need for good Anglo-Irish relations and played down the partition question.

In view of all the earlier campaigning against partition, it was logical that members of the younger generation should become disillusioned with the apparent cynicism of politicians on the issue, and the IRA was able to make a dramatic revival from the near disastrous affects of its attempted collaboration with the Nazis. Buoyed up by new blood, the organisation began a new bombing campaign — this time in Northern Ireland. De Valera again showed that he had no sympathy for the organisation's actions. Following a brief stint in opposition, he returned to power in 1957 and reintroduced internment without trial of IRA suspects, and this was quickly followed by a marked decline in the organisation's activities.

Some weeks before his resignation as Taoiseach to take up the largely ceremonial office of President in June 1959, de Valera was asked at a press conference about his views on partition. Although he had been playing down the issue, he obviously had not changed his mind, especially about the grievance of cutting off nationalists in contiguous areas in which they actually constituted a majority.

'If six of the thirty-two counties can "self-determine" themselves out of the historic national territory, why cannot two counties — Tyrone and Fermanagh, not to speak of areas like Derry City, South Armagh and South Down —

"self-determine" themselves out of the artificial area of the Six Counties.'[80] That was a question that was never satis- factorily answered during de Valera's political career, nor indeed during his lifetime.

CHAPTER SIX

Doing It His Way

Conclusion

Eamon de Valera had a particular style of leadership which, according to his eventual successor Seán Lemass, 'relied upon the force of physical exhaustion to get agreement.' The Chief, as his closer colleagues called him, 'never let a cabinet debate on any subject end with a vote of ministers. He always wanted unanimity and he sought this unanimity by the simple process of keeping the debate going — often till the small hours of the morning, until those who were in the minority, out of sheer exhaustion, conceded the case made by the majority.'[1] As most of the cabinet were republicans who shared his nationalist outlook and all were his own appointees, he almost inevitably got his own way. He was, to use the title of one of his earlier biographers, a *Unique Dictator.*[2]

In no area was his supremacy more apparent than in the field of international relations, where he retained the portfolio of External Affairs for himself throughout the years Fianna Fáil was in power during the 1930s and 1940s. At times he did involve other cabinet members in diplomatic matters, but he never allowed them to get anything like the expertise with which any one of them might challenge him in the field.

The only Irishman, other than himself, to gain international stature in the diplomatic arena was Seán Lester, who became the last Secretary General of the League of Nations during the Second World War. Although Lester served in that position with distinction, the Soviet Union blocked his transfer to the secretariate of the United Nations after the war. Lester then sought to rejoin the Irish Department of External Affairs, but he was shamefully and inexplicably snubbed. Thus the only Irish person with a standing to challenge the Fianna Fáil leader's pre-eminence in diplomatic matters was discarded, with the result that de Valera's own views dominated such affairs.

Paradoxically one of de Valera's most significant achievements having come to power in 1932 was to prove that he had been badly wrong in his evaluation of the Anglo-Irish Treaty back in 1921. He actually admitted in 1932 that he had underestimated the benefits of the Treaty, as he proceeded systematically to use the Statute of Westminster to dismantle unilaterally most of the disagreeable aspects of the 1921 agreement. He managed not only to get the oath, the office of Governor-General, and the right of appeal to the Privy Council abolished, but he was also able to introduce reciprocal citizenship in the Free State and have a new, clearly autochthonous constitution ratified by popular referendum. Yet it would be wrong to suggest that de Valera was primarily responsible for the freedom demonstrated by all those advances. He was not. That freedom already existed as a result of the Treaty and the efforts of the Cumann na nGaedheal governments. What he did was demonstrate its existence. In little over five years he achieved the basic status that he had been seeking back in 1921 with his Document No. 2, with the exception of the removal of the defence provisions of the Treaty, which could not be achieved without the formal approval of Britain.

The defence clauses had been of particular interest to de Valera because those, in effect, negated the Dublin government's theoretical right to remain neutral in a war involving the British, who enjoyed a Treaty right to any Irish facilities they might desire. Obviously, therefore, no enemy of Britain would respect Irish neutrality if the British exercised their right to facilities in Ireland. Back in 1929 de Valera had declared in New York that what he wanted 'above all is the right to be able to remain neutral in case of war and not to be made a naval base' by Britain.[3] Yet, when he set about dismantling the Treaty, the defence clauses were among the last items to be tackled.

There was an astute method to de Valera's approach. By acting unilaterally and firstly securing a firm consfitutional position, he restricted Britain's grounds for seeking some kind of *quid pro quo* for surrendering her rights to Irish facilities. Had he not secured the constitutional position first, he was sure that the British would have insisted that he compromise on his constitutional claims in return for the agreements of April 1938, which abrogated the defence clauses of the Treaty, ended the economic war, and settled British claims of over £100 millions for just £10 millions. As a result only the ending of partition stood in the way of the realisation of Ireland's complete national independence.

Within a week of signing the agreement for the return of the ports, de Valera asked for the help of the American Association for Recognition of the Irish Republic for his efforts to end partition. Over the years he had demonstrated an enormous confidence in the potential of American public support. In fact, he said in 1937 that 'without the moral support of American public opinion the Irish Free State could never have become a reality.' Consequently it was not surprising that he made preparations for a propaganda campaign in the United States as part of an obvious attempt to exploit Britain's need for American help in the event of war with Germany. If sufficient support could be generated in America for the ending of partition, he thought Britain might be persuaded to use her influence to bring about Irish unity in order to promote better Anglo-American relations. The Irish leader therefore made plans for a propaganda tour of the United States with the 'chief aim' of enlisting American support on the partition issue. But that tour had to be cancelled with the outbreak of the Second World War in September 1939.

De Valera immediately announced his intention to remain neutral. To an extent his policy was dictated by selfish national considerations, but that was understandable in view of the blatantly selfish attitude adopted by all the major powers during the international crises of the 1930s, when he approached those issues in what one long-term critic described as 'no petty spirit'. He spoke out forcefully during the Manchurian, Chaco, and Ethiopian conflicts — going so far as to imply his government's willingness to participate in military sanctions. He later admitted that he would have felt compelled to support military measures against Italy had the League called for them during the Ethiopian crisis.

De Valera's main reason for advocating neutrality, therefore, was not inspired by selfishness. He believed in Ireland playing her full part in an ordered international society, and he was prepared to support actions designed to uphold the legitimate aims of the League, but once the major powers refused to honour their obligations under the Covenant, he thought it madness to become involved in a conflict, which had basically resulted from the various powers pursuing their own self-interests. In none of the crises during the 1930s had Britain, France, or the United States been prepared to support the League to the logical extent necessary to ensure the effectiveness of the Covenant. And notwithstanding all the hyperbole, Britain and France did not enter the Second World War to help Poland, as was evidenced by the fact that no real assistance was given to the Poles. Most of the Allied countries, including the United States, did not actually go to war until they were attacked. And de Valera was rightly convinced that it would have been madness for a poor, tiny, divided nation, with little military or economic resources, to become involved voluntarily in such a war, especially when it was likely to lead to civil strife at home.

A secondary consideration was the realisation that remaining neutral would further demonstrate Irish independence in international affairs. Although the country had already attained political independence, this was by no means universally recognised at the time, but would be conclusively proved by steering an independent course in the face of Allied pressure and Axis provocation during the war.

Neutrality had the support of the overwhelming majority of the Irish people, but in later years there would be some questioning of the policy on the reputed grounds that it was indifferent to the real menace of Nazi tyranny, seeing that the Dublin government seemed insistent on remaining neutral even if it meant allowing Hitler to win the war. Yet in a strict sense de Valera's attitude was really one of non-belligerency, rather than neutrality — because his wartime policy was benevolently disposed towards the Allies. For example, the Canadian representative in Dublin reported that even before the United States entered the conflict, Irish authorities had demonstrated that they would 'do almost anything to help us short of involving themselves in the war.'

Of course, de Valera did not openly take his non-belligerency to the same lengths as President Roosevelt who — using the analogy that one would loan a garden hose to a neighbour whose house was on fire, if only to prevent the fire spreading to one's own house — had secured Congressional authorisation for lend-lease, in accordance with which the United States gave war materials to Britain. Some people tried to carry that argument a little further with de Valera by suggesting that he should allow Britain to use Irish ports on the principle that one would surely allow firemen to get out on one's roof in order to put out the fire next door.

'Of course we would,' de Valera responded, 'but that is not the analogy to what we are being asked to do. What we are being asked to do is to set our own house on fire in company with the other house. We have been asked to throw ourselves into the flames — that is what it amounts to.'[4] Convinced that providing bases to any belligerent country would involve Ireland in the war, he resolutely rejected all overtures for facilities.

There was no indication that the Irish leader would ever have been prepared to abandon non-belligerency if an open alliance with the Allies became vital to stop the Nazis, which, of course, presupposes a hypothetical situation that clearly never arose. What did happen was that de Valera provided the Allies with virtually *all* the help he could possibly give them. Admittedly that help, in terms of the overall war effort, was essentially insignificant, but there was very little that a tiny, divided nation like Ireland could do.

As early as 1940 Irish authorities contended that bases in the Twenty-six Counties would be of little use to the Allies as long as the Germans controlled the coast of France, because the safest route for ships destined for, and coming from, Britain was via the North Channel off Northern Ireland, where the British already had bases. Service chiefs in both London and Washington subsequently came to the conclusion not only that the Irish ports — over which Churchill kicked up such a fuss — would be a liability to the Allied war effort, but that no chance should be taken of de Valera joining the Allied war effort because they realised that the Irish could not, in effect, provide any more significant help than was already being given. Yet before the war was over the Irish leader's international reputation would be in tatters and he would be discredited in the eyes of many as a Nazi sympathiser.

The American Minister was responsible for what had happened. He had managed to convince Roosevelt and Churchill that it was necessary to discredit de Valera in order to ensure that the latter would not be able to undermine the post-war peace agreement for selfish political ends. Believing that de Valera's political strength was dependent on exploiting the residual Irish bitterness towards Britain, Gray thought that the Taoiseach would inevitably seek to inject the partition question into international politics by appealing to the expected post-war peace conference to insist upon Irish unity. When this had failed, as it inevitably would, he felt that de Valera would call upon the American people to reject the peace treaty just as he had done in 1919 after the Paris Peace Conference ignored Irish claims. All this raised the dreaded spectre of a repeat of the disaster that surrounded American's rejection of the Versailles Treaty.

Gray's attitude was coloured by his own annoyance at what he thought had been de Valera's cynical manipulation of the anglophobia of the Irish people. 'The anti-British issue is so essential to his political existence that he is unwilling to abandon it,' the American Minister wrote in March 1941. 'He would like Britain to survive, but rather than contribute to her survival with any sacrifice of his political position which he considers synonymous with Ireland's best interests, he would have Ireland go down in general ruins.'[5]

Over the years de Valera had made little effort to mollify

the anglophobia of his people, which he clearly did not share himself. He had admitted, for example, that he dare not publicly give Chamberlain due credit for the Anglo-Irish agreements of April 1938, and during the war he was not openly prepared to admit, what he acknowledged privately, that Britain had a moral position in the conflict. Of course, he had authorised secret co-operation with the British which Gray did not know about in 1941. On learning the following year, after the United States entered the war, the American Minister wrote that Irish co-operation was 'beyond what might reasonably have been believed possible'. Yet he was not satisfied with anything short of complete co-operation, and he never gave the Dublin government due credit for its benevolence, because he thought that Irish neutrality hurt the Allies in two ways — by denying them bases and by allowing Axis representatives to remain in Ireland, where they posed an espionage threat to the Allied war effort.

When Gray tried to get Washington to ask for bases, however, he was told that they would only be a liability, but he did manage to persuade the White House and State Department to ask for the expulsion of Axis representatives, not for the security reasons given, but in order to be able to discredit de Valera in American eyes for being unco-operative. The whole approach was made in such a way as to ensure the Taoiseach's refusal. Then when the affair was publicised in the United States, some sections of the press became almost hysterical and accused de Valera of being a Nazi sympathiser. He furthered that image himself towards the end of the war by formally offering his condolences to the German Minister following Hitler's death. The Taoiseach had apparently been goaded into that action by his annoyance at Gray.

With his reputation seriously tarnished de Valera had to wait before launching his postponed anti-partition campaign. As he waited his government was confronted with its first constitutional challenge from the left wing with the emergence of Seán MacBride's Clann na Poblachta, which won two by-elections in late 1947. Some people equated those victories with the Sinn Féin by-election wins in 1917, and there were predictions that at the next general election the new party would emulate the Sinn Féin showing of 1918. In an obvious move to deny Clann na Poblachta enough time to organise itself properly de Valera called a surprise general election for February 1948.

Declaring that he was ready to take up his anti-partition efforts where those had been interrupted by the war, de Valera announced during the campaign that he would go to the United States to drum up the support of 'public opinion not only of those who have Irish blood in their veins, but of their fellow citizens — men and women — of other races.' To what extent his election tactics were successful must remain a matter for conjecture. On the one hand, the threat from Clann na Poblachta was stunted as that party fared relatively badly at the polls and suffered irreparable damage to its momentum, but Fianna Fáil lost its own majority and de Valera was replaced as Taoiseach by John A. Costello at the head of a coalition government.

In spite of the set back of losing office de Valera went ahead with his planned visit to the United States, where he toured for four weeks before going on to Australia, New Zealand and India. Throughout his travels he decried the injustice of partition. He tried to portray himself as being prepared to lean over backwards to satisfy unionists in Northern Ireland by making it clear that he would be willing to allow them to retain Stormont with its existing powers, provided the authority vested in Westminster was transferred to a central Irish parliament. If the unionists would not accept such a compromise, he contended that they should be bought out. 'We would say to them,' he declared, 'we would prefer that you stay, but if you prefer an outside power we cannot have our unity threatened by your loyalty. If you don't want to be Irish, we are prepared to let you go and compensate you.' He was apparently still thinking of his pre-war plan of transferring Northern Protestants to Britain and possibly replacing them with Roman Catholics of Irish extraction from Britain.

In opposition de Valera showed a distinct hardening of his attitude on the partition question. He went so far as calling for the transfer to the Twenty-six Counties of Counties Fermanagh and Tyrone, which each had anti-partition majorities. Yet while in office he had not asked for the nationalist counties alone, because he said the whole partition question should be solved at the one time. Consequently his call for Tyrone and Fermanagh in 1949 raised some doubts about his sincerity on the issue, not only because he had not asked for the counties earlier, but also because he did not seem to make any effort to get them either having regained power. Kevin Boland, who served in de Valera's last government, wrote that he eventually 'entertained the heretical thought' that de Valera's anti-partition efforts during the world tour 'may have been more a comeback effort in Twenty-six County politics than a real initiative for the establishment of justice and democracy.'[6]

Having taken over as Taoiseach again in 1951 de Valera showed no interest in securing the transfer of the nationalist areas alone. In fact, within a couple of months he revealed that he was pursuing a policy which, to have any prospect of success, necessitated the nationalist areas remaining within Northern Ireland. He advocated securing unity, for instance, by winning over a majority of the people in Northern Ireland. 'About one-third of the people in that area are our supporters and want to have the unity of the country,' he said. 'What you really have to win over is, therefore, the difference between one-third and one half, that is, one-sixth.'

In the following months he played down the partition question as he declared that 'the only one policy' that had any chance of success was 'a policy of trying to establish decent relations between Britain and the Six Counties and ourselves.' Yet he made no concrete suggestions as to how this could be achieved. Indeed, he seemed disinterested in making any progress, except on what would have been his own terms. He was unwilling, for example, to eliminate the discrimination in favour of Roman Catholic and nationalist values in the Twenty-six Counties, but, of course, he seemed to believe that compromising would be a futile gesture.

'Is there anyone foolish enough to think that if we are

going to sacrifice our aspirations that they are going to give up their cry of not an inch?' de Valera once asked in the Dáil. 'For every step we moved towards them, you know perfectly well they would regard it as a sign that we would move another, and they would not be satisfied, in my opinion, unless we went back and accepted the old United Kingdom, a common parliament for the two countries.'[7]

He was probably right. To have eliminated the discrimination against Protestant and unionist values would likely have had no more impact on the unionist desire for retaining ties with Britain than eliminating discrimination against Roman Catholics in the North would have undermined the oppositon to partition in the rest of the island. Yet it would have removed a legimate cause of unionist anxiety and Dublin could, if it wished, have had a stronger base from which to enlist international support for pressurising Britain to hand over the contiguous nationalist areas and insist on the elimination of discrimination against Roman Catholics in what would remain of Northern Ireland.

Of course, de Valera was always more involved with exploiting the propaganda value of the injustices being suffered by nationalists in the Six Counties than in trying to secure the redress of the actual grievances. In fact, he was obviously content to leave the contiguous nationalist areas in the North because that fuelled the fires of anti-partitionism. He really adopted his own variant of the unionist policy of 'not an inch'. Yet David Gray was wrong when he accused him of not wanting to end partition but only desiring to exploit the issue. De Valera did want Irish unity, but on his own terms, which raises the question: What were those terms?

Over the years de Valera developed the acute sense of being able to talk at length without actually committing himself on certain issues. One frustrated Dáil deputy compared that skill to that of a man who sheared a pig — 'he produced a good deal of sound, but no wool.'[8] Having talked too much for his own political good during the Dáil debate that followed the signing of the Anglo-Irish Treaty in 1921, de Valera learned a political lesson about not being too specific at times. He confessed in 1938, for instance, that he was afraid that if he talked a lot he would be 'bound sometime or other to make very serious mistakes.'[9] He seemed particularly reticent about coming forward with a practical plan to end partition.

One guide that the Northern majority had of the kind of Ireland that de Valera was offering them was the constitution of 1937, which called for them to recognise 'the special position of the Roman Catholic Church as the guardian of the Faith professed by the great majority of the citizens.' The unionists would also have to accept that Britain and her institutions would have no constitutional role in Ireland, where Irish would be the first official language, and where divorce would be unconstitutional. As a politician of proven ability to survive, it is difficult to believe that de Valera was ever so naïve to think that the unionists of Northern Ireland would accept that constitution. One is therefore left with the conclusion that the only solution he really wanted was one in which those who would not accept his terms would be transferred to Britain.

It seems inappropriate, however, to end this study of de Valera's quest for full national independence on a sour note, in view of his accomplishments, especially in the years between 1932 and 1945 when he pursued statesmanlike policies of which his fellow countrymen could be truly proud. In that period he conclusively demonstrated the political independence of the Twenty-six Counties, which had always been his primary aim.

Notes

Abbreviations used:

CDP: Canadian Diplomatic Papers, National Archives, Ottawa, Canada.
FDRL: Franklin D. Roosevelt Library, Hyde Park, New York, USA.
des: despatch.
de V.: Eamon de Valera.
DGFP: *Documents on German Foreign Policy.*
MS: Manuscript source.
NLI: National Library of Ireland.
SPO: State Paper Office, Dublin Castle, Dublin.
tel; telegram.
UCD: University College, Dublin.
USNA: National Archives of the United States of America, Washington, D.C.

PRELUDE
1. de V. to Griffith, 6.3.20, DE2/245.
2. Dáil, *Private Sessions,* 13.
3. Seanad, *Debates,* 15:938.
4. Dáil, *Private Sessions,* 137.
5. *Ibid., Debate on the Treaty,* 8.
6. Rex Taylor, *Michael Collins,* 141.
7. R. Erskine Childers, 'Diary', 6.12.21, R. E. Childers Papers, Trinity College, Dublin.
8. Barton to author, 2.9.69, and 1.10.69.
9. de V., statement, 1.5.22, *Irish Independent,* 2.5.22.
10. de V., speech, Enniscorthy, 2.8.36.
11. Childers, 'Diary', 22.5.22.
12. de V., to Cathal Ó Murchadha, 13.9.22.
13. C. S. Andrews, *Dublin Made Me,* 247.
14. Michael McInerny, 'Gerry Boland's Story', *Irish Times,* 10.10.68.
15. Ó Faoláin, *De Valera* (1939), 111.
16. Seanad, *Debates,* 15:938.
17. Dáil, *Private Sessions,* 137.
18. Michael Hayes, 'Dáil Éireann and the Irish Civil War', *Studies,* Spring 1969.
19. Phillips, *The Revolution in Ireland.*

CHAPTER ONE
1. Dulanty to Thomas, 22.3.32, correspondence relating to Anglo-Irish negotiations of 1932 in S. 6298, SPO.
2. Thomas to de V., 23.3.32.
3. de V. to Thomas, 5.4.32.
4. Dáil *Debates,* 41:927.
5. *Ibid.,* 568-77; 1090-91.
6. *Ibid.,* 46:2098-99.
7. O'Kelly, 'The Irish Land Annuities,' *New Outlook,* 161:38.
8. Chamberlain, memo., 8.3.32, Fanning, *Irish Department of Finance,* 277.
9. Dáil *Debates,* 42:1688-93.
10. O'Kelly, 38.
11. Dáil *Debates,* 42:1690.

12. Hansard, *Debates,* 276:683.
13. Thomas, *My Story,* 188.
14. Hansard, *Debates,* 276:683.
15. de V. to Thomas, 16.6.32.
16. Speech in *Seanad,* 25.5.32, Moynihan, 213.
17. Seanad *Debates,* 15:938.
18. Report of meeting, 5.10.32, S. 6298, SPO.
19. MacNeill to de V., 26.4.32.
20. de V. to MacNeill, 30.4.32.
21. de V. to MacNeill, 7.5.32.
22. Harkness, 'Mr de Valera's Dominion,' 209.
23. Report of meeting, 15.7.32, S. 6298, SPO.
24. Report of meetings of 14-15.10. 32, S. 6298, SPO.
25. Inskip, speech, Stranraer, 4.8.32, *The Times,* 5.8.32.
26. speech, 10.7.35.
27. Lynch to editor, *Kerryman,*   6.8.32.
28. *United Irishman,* 10.9.32.
29. Árd Fheis address, 8.11.32, Moynihan, 230.
30. Advertisement, *Kerryman,* 14.1.32.
31. Advertisement, *Kerryman,* 21.1.32.
32. Longford and O'Neill, 275.
33. de V. to Thomas, 29.11.32.
34. *New York Times,* 16.12.32.
35. *Ibid.,* 18.2.33.
36. Connolly, 'Memoirs', MS. 258.
37. *Ibid.*
38. Speech, 27.3.34, *New York Times,* 28.3.34.
39. McDowell, tel. 7, 28.3.34, USNA.
40. Hull to McDowell, 29.3.34.
41. *Manchester Guardian,* 13.9.34.
42. *Economist,* 3.11.34.
43. Harkness, 'Mr de Valera's Dominion', 213.
44. Dáil *Debates,* 64:1279-80.
45. Harkness, 220.
46. de V. to McGarrity, Sept. 1933, Cronin, *McGarrity Papers,* 156.
47. de V. to McGarrity, 31.1.34.
48. *Ibid.*
49. Speech, Enniscorthy, 2.8.36.

CHAPTER TWO
 1. see Dwyer, *De Valera's Darkest Hour.*
 2. Many of de Valera's speeches were conveniently collected in de V., *Peace and War.*
 3. Except where noted the following press comments were all dated, 27.9.32.
 4. Connolly, 234.
 5. *Ibid.*
 6. *The Times* (London), 28.9.32.; *New York Herald-Tribune,* 28.9.32.
 7. de V., *Peace and War,* 15-20.
 8. *New York Times,* 25-26.11.32.
 9. *Ibid.,* 26.11.32.
10. Wunsz King, *China and the League of Nations,* 51.
11. *New York Times,* 8.12.32.
12. Connolly, 238.
13. de V., *Peace and War,* 21-26.

14. Speech, 18.9.34, *Peace and War*, 32-34.
15. Speech, 21.9.34, *Ibid.*, 27-31.
16. Speech, 19.9.34, *Ibid.*, 35-38.
17. *New York Times*, 20.9.34.
18. *Irish Press*, 23.8.35.
19. Speech, 12.9.35, de V., *Peace and War*, 39-43.
20. *Ibid.*, 44-48.
21. Hoare's speech, 11.9.35.
22. de V., *Peace and War*, 49-53.
23. Speech, 12.9.35., de V., *Peace and War*, 39-43.
24. Speech, 4.10.35.
25. *Round Table*, 26:131.
26. Speech at Fianna Fáil Árd Fheis, 12.10.37, Moynihan, 330-43.
27. Churchill, *Second World War*, 1:177.
28. Dáil *Debates*, 62:2656.
29. Churchill, 1:176.
30. Dáil *Debates*, 62:2655.
31. de V., *Peace and War*, 54-59.
32. Manning, *The Blueshirts*, 201.
33. McInerney, *Peadar O'Donnell*, 183.
34. Dáil *Debates*, 65:835.
35. O'Brien, 'Ireland in International Affairs', 117.
36. Lester, diary, 20.5.37, Barcroft, 'The International Civil Servant'.228.
37. *Ibid.*
38. de V., *Peace and War*, 60-64.
39. Dáil *Debates*, 69:2266.
40. Lapointe, memo., 31.3.39, Riddell, *Documents on Canadian Foreign Policy*, 235-36.

CHAPTER THREE
1. Dáil *Debates*, 62:2660.
2. *Ibid.*, 72:691.
3. Speech, 4.3.32, de V., *Recent Speeches*, 9-14.
4. *Ibid.*
5. Broadcast to USA, 12.2.33, *Ibid.*, 57-59.
6. Dáil *Debates*, 46:192.
7. Seanad *Debates*, 15:1320-21.
8. *Irish Times*, 29.9.32.
9. Rumpf and Hepburn, *Nationalism and Socialism*, 121.
10. *Ibid.*, 115-20; Hoctor, *History of the Department of Agriculture*, 166-98.
11. de V., memo., 17.9.37, Longford and O'Neill, 310.
12. de V. to MacDonald, 24.11.37, cabinet conclusion, 45 (37) 6 of 2.3.38, Younger, *A State of Disunion*, 302.
13. *Ibid.*
14. MacDonald, memo of conversation with de V., 14.1.37, MacMahon, 'Malcolm MacDonald and Anglo-Irish Relations', 72-80.
15. MacDonald, memo., n.d., Cab. 27, 527, ISC (32) 128, *Ibid.*, 111.
16. MacDonald, memo., 14.1.37.
17. MacDonald, memo., 6.10.37, Cab. 24, 271, CP 228 (37), *Ibid.*, 94.
18. Cudahy, des. 4, 24.8.37.
19. Cudahy, tel. 1, 14.1.38. USNA.
20. Cabinet conclusion 2 (38) 4 of 26.1.38, Younger, 303.
21. *Ibid.*
22. *Ibid.*

23. Longford and O'Neill, 314.
24. *Ibid.*, 315.
25. Cab. 27, 642, INS (38), MacMahon, 127.
26. Chamberlain's diary, 23.1.38, Feiling, *Chamberlain*, 310.
27. Cudahy to Roosevelt, 22.1.38, FDRL.
28. Cudahy, des. 51, 24.1.38.
29. Cudahy to Roosevelt, 22.1.38.
30. Walshe to Gallagher, 4.3.38, Nunan Papers, MS 18,367, NLI.
31. de V. to Roosevelt, 25.1.38.
32. Roosevelt to Cudahy, 9.2.38.
33. Longford and O'Neill, 322.
34. Cabinet conclusion, 11 (38) 8 of 9.3.38, Younger, 306.
35. Dulanty to Walshe, 14.3.38, Longford and O'Neill, 323.
36. Cudahy, tel. 4, 14.3.38.
37. Dulanty to Walshe, 15.3.38, Longford and O'Neill, 323.
38. Cabinet conclusion, 19 (38) 6 of 13.4.38, Younger, 307-8.
39. de V. to Roosevelt, 22.4.38.
40. Cudahy to Roosevelt, 29.4.38.
41. Cudahy to Roosevelt, 26.4.38.
42. Cudahy to Hill, 2.5.38.
43. Connolly, 'Memoirs'.
44. Speech in Dáil, 27.4.38, Moynihan, 350.
45. *Irish Times*, 9.6.38.
46. Lester, diary, 29.4.38, Barcroft.
47. Dáil *Debates,* 72.699.
48. Speech, 12.9.38, de V., *Peace and War,* 67-68.
49. *Ibid.*
50. Inskip, memo. of conversation, 8.9.38, MacMahon, 209.
51. Diana Cooper, *The Light of Common Day,* 243.
52. de V. to Chamberlain, 15.9.38, Feiling, 364.
53. MacMahon, 'Malcolm MacDonald', 217.
54. Lord de la Warr's report of conversation with de Valera, MacMahon, 'Ireland, the Dominions and the Munich Crisis', 31.
55. *Ibid.*, 33.
56. de V., *Peace and War,* 69-75.
57. *The Times* (London), 28.9.38.
58. de V., *Peace and War,* 76-80.
59. Speech, 27.4.38, Moynihan, 351-352.
60. Transcript of interview, Moynihan, 359-62.
61. *Time,* 31.10.38.
62. Cudahy, des. 173, 25.11.38.
63. Cudahy, des. 159, 20.10.38.
64. Speech in Seanad, 7.2.39, Moynihan, 367.
65. Seanad *Debates,* 39:1539.
66. Ó Faoláin, *De Valera* (1939), 156.
67. Dáil *Debates,* 39:517-18.
68. Whyte, *Church and State in Modern Ireland,* 47-48.
69. Speech in Seanad, 7.2.39, Moynihan, 372.
70. Ó Faoláin, 156.
71. Speech in Seanad, 7.2.39, Moynihan, 375.
72. *Ibid.*, 372.
73. Speech, Geneva, 21.9.34, de V., *Peace and War,* 27-31.
74. Speech, Fianna Fáil Árd Fheis, November 1939.
75. Speech in Seanad, 7.2.39, Moynihan, 371.

76. Moynihan, 376-79.
77. Cudahy, report of meeting with de Valera, des. 214, 6.4.39.
78. Cudahy (per McVeagh), des. 213, 3.4.39.
79. Cudahy to Roosevelt, 6.4.39.
80. Broadcast to USA, 25.12.39.
81. William A. Bullitt, report of conversation with de Valera in Paris, 8.3.39,
    Bullitt, tel. 434, 9.3.39, USNA.
82. Farley, *Jim Farley's Story,* 194-95.

CHAPTER FOUR

1. For wartime relations between Germany and Ireland, see Carter,
   Shamrock and Swastika, and Stephan, *Spies in Ireland.*
2. Hempel, tel. 85, 8.10.39, *DGFP,* 8:241.
3. MacMahon, 'Malcolm MacDonald', 55.
4. Maffey, report of meeting with de Valera, 14.9.39, Bethell, 239-41.
5. Maffey, report of conversation with de Valera, 21.10.39.
6. Maffey, report of conversation with de Valera, 14.9.39.
7. For Ango-Irish relations during the war, see Carroll, *Ireland in the War
   Years.*
8. Churchill to First Sea Lord, 24.9.39, Churchill, *The Second World War,*
   1:729.
9. Cudahy, des. 306, 7.12.39.
10. *Ibid.,* Cudahy to Roosevelt, 7.12.39.
11. For relations between United States and Ireland during the war, see
    Dwyer, *Irish Neutrality and the USA.*
12. Cabinet conclusion, WM 168 (40) 5 of 16.6.40.
13. Warlimont, *Inside Hitler's Headquarters,* 106.
14. *Irish Press,* 5.7.40.
15. *New York Times,* 6.7.40.
16. *Ibid.,* 6.11.40; *New York Herald Tribune,* 7.11.40.
17. Speech in Dáil, 7.11.40, Moynihan, 450.
18. Gray, tel. 99, 10.11.40.
19. Speech in Dáil, 7.11.40, Moynihan, 451.
20. Speech, Drogheda, 28.2.54.
21. de V., tel. to J. J. Reilly, *New York Times,* 10.11.40.
22. Interview with W. Carroll, 19.11.40, de V., *Ireland's Stand,* 28-33.
23. *Congressional Record,* 1940, 86:A6590-91.
24. see O'Dwyer, *Counsel for the Defence.*
25. Kelly, des. 33, 15.11.40, CDP.
26. Gray, tel. 99, 10.11.40.
27. Maffey to Churchill, 25.11.40.
28. Churchill to Cranborne, 22.11. 40, Churchill, 2:690.
29. Hempel, tel. 320, 17.6.40, *DGFP* 9:601-3.
29. Hempel, tel. 320, 17.6.40, *DGFP* 9:601-3.
30. Hempel, tel. 437, 31.7.40, *Ibid.,* 10:379-80.
31. see also Hempel, tel. 324, 19.6.40. *Ibid.,* 9:637-40; tel. 347, 1.7.40, *Ibid.,*
    10:89-90.
32. William J. Donovan, memo., n.d., Box 4 President's Secretary's File,
    Ireland folder, FDRL.
33. For a more detailed treatment, see Dwyer, 'The Ambassador Who Spoke
    to Ghosts', *Sunday Press,* 3-17.2.80.
34. Terry de Valera to editor, *Irish Times,* 10.9.79, and 10.10.79; War Cabinet
    conclusion 310 (40) 6 of 27.12.40; see also Rosenberg, 268.
35. *New York Times,* 26.12.40.

36. *Ibid.*, 27.12.40; text of broadcast in de V., *Ireland's Stand,* 34-39.
37. Gray to Roosevelt, 22.1.41.
38. Churchill to Roosevelt, 13.12.40.
39. Carroll, 82.
40. Maffey's report, 20.1.41, *Irish Times,* 23.5.75.
41. Churchill to Cranborne, 17.1.41 and 31.1.41, Churchill, 3:611, 615.
42. Brennan, 'War-Time Mission', *Irish Press,* 7.5.58.
43. Lindbergh, *Wartime Journals,* 495.
44. Speech, Cork, 14.12.41, Moynihan, 461-62.
45. Kearney to N. A. Robertson, 20.2.42, CDP.
46. Kearney, des. 110, 12.8.43.
47. de Vere White, 'Lord Rugby Remembers', *Irish Times,* 4.7.62.
48. MacEvoy, 'Canadian Irish Relations', 214.
49. Rosenberg, 57.
50. Carroll, 124.
51. Carter, 41.
52. For in-depth treatment of the American note, see Dwyer, *Irish Neutrality and the USA,* 179-99.
53. Gray, tel. 28, 21.2.44.
54. Carroll, 142.
55. Speech, Cavan, 27.2.44.
56. *Fort Worth Star Telegram,* 17.3.44.
57. Smyllie, 'Unneutral Neutral Éire', 324.
58. *New York Times,* 16.11.44.
59. Gray, memo. of conversation with de Valera, 30.4.45, and with Walshe, 1.5.45, Gray Papers, FDRL.
60. San Francisco *Leader,* 19.5.45.
61. *New York Times,* 4.5.45.
62. Kearney, des. 55, 14.5.45.
63. de V. to Brennan, Whit-Monday, 1945, Longford and O'Neill, 411.
64. Gray to Eleanor Roosevelt, 13.4.45.
65. de V. to Brennan, Whit-Monday, 1945.
66. Kearney to Robertson, 22.5.45.
67. Dwyer, *Irish Neutrality,* 210.
68. Garrett, des. 2402, 7.8.47, USNA.

CHAPTER FIVE

1. Árd Fheis address, 22.6.48.
2. Gray to Norman H. Davis, 28.10.41.
3. Gray to Roosevelt, 8.4.40.
4. Gray to Welles, 23.6.40.
5. Cabinet conclusion, 25.6.40.
6. MacDonald's report, 27.6.40.
7. Gerald Boland, MS, supplied by Kevin Boland.
8. Chamberlain to de V., 29.6.40.
9. *The Observer* (London), 30.6.40.
10. Mulcahy, memo. of conversation, 2.7.40, Mulcahy Papers, UCD.
11. Mulcahy, memo., 5.7.40.
12. Gray to Roosevelt, 28.6–4.7.40.
13. Dáil *Debates,* 120:714.
14. de V. to Chamberlain, 4.7.40.
15. de V. tel. to J. J. Reilly, *New York Times,* 10.11.40.
16. Hempel, tel. 787, 7.12.40, *DGFP,* 11:805.
17. Speech, Castlebar, 19.4.41, Moynihan, 459.

18. For a deeper treatment of the conscription crisis, see Dwyer, *Irish Neutrality*, 122-28.
19. de V. to Gray, 25.5.41.
20. de V. to Churchill, 25.5.41, Moynihan, 459.
21. Gray to Roosevelt, 28.7.41, Moynihan, 459.
22. Hull, *Memoirs*, 1354.
23. Statement, 27.1.42, Moynihan, 465.
24. Gray, memo. of conversation, 3.6.43.
25. Gray, memo. of conversation with Winant, Attlee, Cranborne, Maffey, and Morrison, 17.11.42.
26. Gray's efforts are covered in more detail in Dwyer, *Irish Neutrality*, 160-200.
27. Gray to Robert Stewart, 22.12. 43.
28. Gray to Winant, 7.1.44.
29. *Ibid*.
30. Gray to Roosevelt, 2.6.44.
31. Speech in Dáil, 24.7.46, Moynihan, 485.
32. Speech in Dáil, 25.7.46, *Ibid,*. 485-90.
33. *Irish Press*, 8.11.47.
34. Speech, 17.3.47.
35. *Irish Press*, 21.6.47.
36. Dáil *Debates*, 107:80-81.
37. Gray, memo. of conversation, 26.6.47.
38. Dáil *Debates*, 107:84-85.
39. *Ibid.*, 97:2573.
40. *Ibid.*, 107:86-87.
41. *Irish Press*, 29.1.48.
42. *Ibid.*, 11.3.48.
43. de V., radio broadcast, Chicago, 21.3.48, *Irish Press supplement*, 'With de Valera in America and Australia.'
44. de V., broadcast, Chicago, 21.3.48.
45. Press conference, New York, 8.3.48.
46. Radio broadcast, Chicago, 21.3.48.
47. Speech, Detroit, 22.3.48.
48. Speech, New York, 3.4.48, Moynihan, 504.
49. Speech, Providence, R.I., 25.3.48.
50. Speech, Boston, 28.3.48.
51. Speech, 31.3.48.
52. Address to Massachusetts State Legislature, 29.3.48.
53. *Ibid.*
54. *Irish Press*, 1.5.48.
55. *Ibid.*, 19.5.48.
56. *Ibid.*, 19.6.48.
57. Keating, *A Place Among the Nations*, 112.
58. Dáil *Debates*, 112:950, 954.
59. Speech, Clonmellon, 8.8.48.
60. Speech, Ennis, *Irish Press*, 16.8.48.
61. Speech, Dublin, 7.2.48, Moynihan, 523.
62. *Irish Press*, 28.2.49.
63. *Ibid.*, 2.5.49.
64. *Ibid.*, 18.8.49.
65. O'Brien, 'Ireland in International Affairs', 124.
66. *Irish Times*, 10.3.48.
67. *New York Times*, 30.3.50.

68. *Ibid.*, 31.3.50.
69. *Irish Press*, 15.3.51.
70. Speech, Slough, *Ibid.*, 19.3.51.
71. Press conference, London, 16.3.51.
72. *Ibid.*
73. Speech, Slough, 18.3.51.
74. Moynihan, 541-44.
75. *New York Times*, 15.8.51.
76. *Ibid.*, 16.8.51
77. *Ibid.*
78. Speech, 11.9.52, Blanchard, *The Irish and Catholic Power*, 358.
79. Eisenhower's speech was quoted by Gray in preface of Carson, *Ulster and the Irish Republic*, ix.

CHAPTER SIX
1. Lemass, interview, *Irish Press*, 3.2.69.
2. Ryan, *Unique Dictator: A Study of Eamon de Valera*.
3. *New York Times*, 11.12.29.
4. Dáil *Debates*, 84:1913-14.
5. Gray to Sumner Welles, 7.3.41.
6. Kevin Boland, *Up Dev*, 7.
7. *Ibid.*, 144.
8. Dáil *Debates*, 97:2652.
9. *Ibid.*, 71:439.

Bibliography

This bibliography is intended only *to provide additional information on, and a cross-reference to, works cited in the book. It does not purport to be a list of works consulted.*

MANUSCRIPT SOURCES:

Canadian Diplomatic Papers, National Archives, Ottawa, Canada.

R. Erskine Childers Papers, Trinity College, Dublin.

Frank Gallagher Papers, National Library of Ireland, Dublin.

David Gray Papers, Franklin D. Roosevelt Library, Hyde Park, New York

David Gray Papers, Western Institute of Research, Laramie, Wyoming.

Joseph McGarrity Papers, National Library of Ireland, Dublin.

Patrick McGilligan Papers, University College, Dublin.

Mary MacSwiney Papers, University College, Dublin.

Richard Mulcahy Papers, University College, Dublin.

Seán Nunan Papers, National Library of Ireland, Dublin.

Official Files of the President of the Executive Council and Taoiseach's Office, State Paper Office, Dublin Castle, Dublin.

Franklin D. Roosevelt Papers, Franklin D. Roosevelt Library, Hyde Park, New York.

United States Diplomatic Papers, National Archives, Washington, D.C.

NEWSPAPERS AND PERIODICALS:

Chicago Tribune, Daily Express, Daily Herald, Economist, The Evening Standard, Fort-Worth Star-Telegram, Irish Independent, Irish Press, Irish Times, Irish World (New York), *Kerryman, Manchester Guardian, Montreal Star, New York Herald-Tribune, New York Times, New Chronicle, Round Table,* San Francisco *Leader, Sunday Press, The Times, Time, United Irishman.*

Andrews, C. S., *Dublin Made Me,* Dublin & Cork, 1979.

Barcroft, Stephen A., 'The International Civil Servant: The League of Nations Career of Seán Lester, 1929-1947', Ph.D. thesis, Trinity College, Dublin.

Bethell, Nicholas, *The War Hitler Won,* London, 1972.

Blanchard, Paul, *The Irish and Catholic Power: An American Interpretation,* New York, 1953.

Brennan, Robert, 'My War-Time Mission in Washington', *Irish Press,* 28 April–17 May 1958.

Carroll, Joseph T., *Ireland in the War Years, 1939-1945,* Newton Abbot, 1975.

Carson, William A., *Ulster and the Irish Republic,* Belfast, 1956.

Carter, Carolle J., *The Shamrock and the Swastika,* Palo Alto, 1977.

Churchill, Winston S., *The Second World War,* 6 vols., London, 1948-54.

Connolly, Joseph, 'Memoirs', MS., in possession of Fr J. Anthony Gaughan.

Cooper, Diana, *The Light of Common Day,* Boston, 1959.

de Valera, Eamon, *Ireland's Stand: Being a selection of the Speeches of Eamon de Valera during the War,* Dublin, 1946.

——, *Peace and War: Speeches by Mr de Valera on International Affairs,* Dublin, 1944.

——, *Recent Speeches and Broadcasts,* Dublin, 1933.

——, *Speeches and Statements by Eamon de Valera, 1917-1973,* ed. by Maurice Moynihan, Dublin, 1980.

Dwyer, T. Ryle, 'The Ambassador Who Spoke to Ghosts', *Sunday Press,* 3-17 February 1980.

——, *Eamon de Valera,* Dublin, 1980.

——, *De Valera's Darkest Hour, 1919-1932,* Dublin and Cork, 1982.

——, *Irish Neutrality and the USA, 1939-1947,* Dublin, 1977.

——, *Michael Collins and the Treaty: His Differences with de Valera,* Dublin and Cork, 1981.

Fanning, Ronan, *The Irish Department of Finance,* Dublin, 1978.

Farley, James A., *Jim Farley's Story,* New York, 1948.

Feiling, Keith, *The Life of Neville Chamberlain,* London, 1946.

Harkness, D. W., 'Mr de Valera's Dominion: Irish Relations with Britain and the Commonwealth, 1932-1938', *Journal of Commonwealth Political Studies,* 8 (November 1970), 206-27.

Hoctor, D., *The Department's Story: A History of the Department of Agriculture,* Dublin, 1971.

Hull, Cordell, *The Memoirs of Cordell Hull,* New York, 1948.

Keating, Richard, *The Formation of Irish Foreign Policy*, Dublin, 1973.

——, *A Place Among the Nations*, Dublin, 1978.

King, Wunsz, *China and the League of Nations: The Sino-Japanese Controversy*, New York, 1965.

Lindberg, Charles A., *The Wartime Journals of Charles A. Lindberg*, New York, 1970.

Longford, Earl of, and O'Neill, Thomas P., *Eamon de Valera*, Dublin, 1970.

McEvoy, Fred, 'Canadian-Irish Relations during the Second World War', *Journal of Imperial and Commonwealth History*, 7 (January 1977), 206-26.

McInerney, Michael, *Peadar O'Donnell*, Dublin, 1974.

MacMahon, Deirdre, 'Ireland, the Dominions and the Munich Crisis', *Irish Studies in International Affairs*, 1 (1979), 30-37.

——, 'Malcolm MacDonald and Anglo-Irish Relations', M.A. thesis, University College, Dublin.

Manning, Maurice, *The Blueshirts*, Dublin, 1970.

Moynihan, Maurice, see de Valera, Eamon.

O'Brien, Conor Cruise, 'Ireland in International Affairs', *Conor Cruise O'Brien Introduces Ireland*, ed. O. Dudley Edwards, London, 1969.

O'Dwyer, Paul, *Counsel for the Defence: The Autobiography of Paul O'Dwyer*, New York, 1979.

Ó Faoláin, Seán, *De Valera*, London, 1939.

O'Kelly, Seán T., 'The Irish Land Annuities', *New Outlook*, 161 (December 1932), 36-40.

O'Sullivan, Donal, *The Irish Free State and Its Senate*, London, 1940.

Riddell, Walter, A., ed., *Documents on Canadian Foreign Policy*, Toronto, 1962.

Rosenberg, Joseph Louis, 'America and the Neutrality of Ireland, 1939-41', Ph.D. thesis, University of Iowa, 1976.

Rumpf, E., and Hepburn, A. C., *Nationalism and Socialism in Twentieth-Century Ireland*, Liverpool, 1977.

Ryan, Desmond, *Unique Dictator: A Study of Eamon de Valera*, London, 1936.

Smyllie, Robert M., 'Unneutral Neutral Eire', *Foreign Affairs*, 24 (January 1946), 317-26.

Stephan, Enno, *Spies in Ireland*, London, 1963.

Taylor, Rex, *Michael Collins*, London, 1958.

Thomas, J. H., *My Story*, London, 1937.

Warlimont, Walter, *Inside Hitler's Headquarters, 1939-45*, New York, 1964.

White, T. de Vere, 'Lord Rugby Remembers', *Irish Times*, 3-5 July 1962.

Younger, Carlton, *A State of Disunion*, London, 1972.

Index

204

MORE MERCIER TITLES

Michael Collins and The Treaty
His Differences with de Valera
T. RYLE DWYER

To Michael Collins the signing of the Treaty between Ireland and Britain in 1921 was a 'Stepping Stone'. Eamon de Valera called it 'Treason'.

The controversy surrounding this Treaty is probably the single most important factor in the history of this country, not only because it led to the Civil War of 1922-1923 but also because the basic differences between the country's two main political parties stem from the dispute.

T. Ryle Dwyer not only takes an in-depth look at the characters and motivations of the two main Irish protagonists but also gives many insights into the views and ideas of the other people involved on both sides of the Irish Sea.

This book is not only the story of Michael Collins' role in the events surrounding the Treaty, but it is also the story of his differences with Eamon de Valera which were to have tragic consequences for the nation.

The Shooting of Michael Collins
Murder or Accident?

JOHN M. FEEHAN

When the first and second editions of this book appeared they sold out instantly and caused a newspaper controversy which lasted many months.

In this third edition the author has rewritten large sections of the book incorporating new and rather startling information which came his way.

Was Michael Collins killed by an accident of war or was he ruthlessly murdered? Both of these possibilities are calmly and carefully examined by the author, who has rejected the traditional theory that he was killed as a result of a ricochet rifle bullet and leans towards the possibility that he was shot by a Mauser pistol.

This new, updated and rewritten edition is sure to arouse exceptional and absorbing interest in this baffling and bewildering mystery.

Brother Against Brother

LIAM DEASY

Brother against Brother is Liam Deasy's moving and sensitive account of the Civil War — Ireland's greatest tragedy.

He tells in detail of the Republican disillusionment with the Truce, and later with the Treaty; how the Civil War began; how the Republicans were hopelessly outnumbered and hunted in the hills like wild animals before they were finally broken and defeated.

For the first time Liam Deasy recalls the circumstances surrounding his much criticised order appealing to his comrades to call off the Civil War — an order which saved the lives of hundreds of prisoners.

In a special chapter he recounts his involvement in the ambush at Béalnabláth where his close friend, Michael Collins, met his death.

Liam Deasy was one of the greatest military leaders thrown up by the Revolution and he writes without bitterness or malice, but with humility and understanding towards all. He gives us a rare and profound insight into the brutal, suicidal war that set father against son and brother against brother.